"Everything the Traffickers don't want you to know is in this book. The tragic reality is most of those caught in modern day slavery are minors. This book is a must-read in learning how to join the fight against human trafficking and how to identify it, protect yourself and your peers."

Shayne Moore, author of *Refuse To Do Nothing*
Founder and Editor-in-Chief at Redbud Writers Guild

"*Slavery in the Land of the Free* is the book I wish I'd had: clear, informative, and compelling, it lays out what we need to know, and what we need to do to be a part of the solution. We dare not look away. I'm so grateful to Theresa Flores and PeggySue Wells for not only telling a story, but giving us tools to make any person—and every person—a Freedom Fighter."

Bronwyn Lea
Award-winning blogger and writer

"Flores writes in a way that allows students the opportunity to learn about and understand the various forms of human trafficking. Each chapter concludes with a summary and call to action that provides students with the ability to get involved and become cognitive of their surroundings in a way that keeps themselves and their communities safer. *Slavery in the Land of the Free* is the introductory to human trafficking that middle and high school students need."

Kacey Long
Human Trafficking and Social Justice Institute
University of Toledo

ISBN: 978-0-9893419-8-1
Library of Congress Control Number: 2016932609

Printed in the United States of America

Requests for information should be addressed to:
Ampelon Publishing
PO Box 140675
Boise, ID 83714

To order other Ampelon Publishing products, visit us on the web at:
www.ampelonpublishing.com

Cover design: Jared Swafford — SwingFromTheRafters.com
Cover photography: Chris Joel Campbell

Printed in the United States of America on post-consumer recycled paper

SLAVERY
IN THE LAND
OF THE FREE

A STUDENT'S GUIDE TO
MODERN DAY SLAVERY

THERESA FLORES
PEGGYSUE WELLS

To my dear my Coalition Sisters! Thanks for helping make my mission come true.

αρ

TABLE OF CONTENTS

INTRODUCTION

SLAVERY IN THE LAND OF THE FREE

THE WORD *slavery* confuses most readers. We've not heard this word used in the United States since slavery became illegal in the 1800's, and later in the 1960's when every citizen was granted the right to vote. Banished from our everyday language, slavery is a term typically only found in textbooks.

Then the phrases *modern day slavery, sex slave, white slavery* and *human trafficking* surfaced.

Today there are more slaves in the world than any other time in history. Not legal in any nation on the globe, slavery is a growing part of the culture experienced by American teens and pre-teens. Their peers and siblings are the victims.

- How does slavery exist?
- Who is at risk?
- What effect does this modern phenomena have on culture?

• What can we do to stop human trafficking?

These questions and more are answered in this book. Chapters are illustrated by the true stories of victims and their families whose lives have been tragically altered and, too often, bitterly lost.

Because people dared to passionately care about others, slavery was abolished once before. Though the enslavement of humans has taken a new and more insidious form, slavery can once again be stopped. In the United States and around the world, people can be free and enjoy their right to life, liberty, and the pursuit of happiness.

By becoming aware of the condition of others, we can make a difference. We can change the world.

CHAPTER ONE

WHAT IS HUMAN TRAFFICKING?

IN THIS CHAPTER:

- HUMAN TRAFFICKING IN EVERY NATION
- DEFINITION OF HUMAN TRAFFICKING
- TRAFFICKING TAKES MANY FORMS

Have the courage to say no. Have the courage to face the truth. Do the right thing because it is right. These are the magic keys to living your life with integrity.
— W. Clement Stone

TWELVE-YEAR-OLD CARRIE was a smart girl taking classes for gifted and talented students. One day as she walked home from middle school, a man in a fancy car drove up beside her and told her she was pretty. Though she didn't tell her parents about him, every day for six months he met her after school and they talked. He bought her small gifts and made her feel special. After six months she finally agreed to get into his car.

When the door shut, Carrie's life changed forever. The man who she thought was her boyfriend drove her far from home. He took away her identity by changing her name, instructing what clothes she could wear, when she could eat, and didn't permit her to contact her family. For the next five years, he prostituted Carrie to more than 100 men each month. Taken from state to state, there was no place for her to run, and she was without hope for rescue. She thought he loved her but she hated the things he made her do. Although Carrie was a United States citizen, in the land of liberty she was no longer free. This all-American pre-teen was a slave.

EVERY NATION IN THE WORLD

What do you think of when you hear the words *slavery* or *human trafficking*? These two terms are interchangeable and describe the vilest form of abuse by one human to another.

When you think of human trafficking, do you envision a little boy in India making rugs for 12 hours a day, given one small bowl of rice to eat, and paid nothing while he works off a family debt? Do you think of a young Egyptian girl sold as a maid to a rich family in another country, only to be locked in a room day in and day out, forced to have sexual relations with the male members of the household? Do you imagine children stolen from their homes and constrained to work on cocoa plantations?

What about a nine-year-old making soccer balls to be sold in the United States and beaten if he does not meet an impossible quota each day? Do you see a four-year-old girl in Cambodia for hire to rich tourists for sex? Or a poverty-stricken young man who is promised a wonderful job in another country only to arrive and find that he is hopelessly indebted to the new employer for his passage?

Yes, these common forms of slavery happen every day and in every country. People in the United States live in comfortable homes, envisioning that slavery is long over because it was eradicated in 1865. However, over 27 million people are trafficked each year world-wide and over 50 percent of victims who are enslaved are children.

Human trafficking plagues America as much, and more, than it does underdeveloped nations. The United States is a top destination for victims of human trafficking. Brought into the nation that calls itself the land of the free, victims are forced to work illegally in households, on farms, in food service jobs, on construction sites, and in massage parlors. Approximately 17,500 people are trafficked into the United States, primarily to be prostituted while another 300,000 American children are at risk of being trafficked in the United States. Prostitution of a person under the age of 18 is a form of modern day slavery.

U.S. CITIES WITH THE HIGHEST CHILD TRAFFICKING[1]

SEATTLE, WA

PORTLAND, OR

SACRAMENTO, CA

TOLEDO, OH

ATLANTA, GA

IT HAPPENS IN YOUR COMMUNITY AND IN EVERY ZIP CODE.

MODERN DAY SLAVERY INCLUDES:

• LABOR
• SEX TRAFFICKING OF CHILDREN AND ADULTS
• DEBT BONDAGE

- DOMESTIC SLAVERY
- CHILD LABOR
- CHILD SOLDIERS
- CHILD BRIDES
- ORGAN TRAFFICKING
- SOME INTERNATIONAL ADOPTIONS
- PROSTITUTION

Traffickers gain complete control over a person's identity or individuality through mental, physical, or emotional abuse. Usually all three.

Traffickers do not function by a moral compass as their victims do. Traffickers ruthlessly use threats, manipulation, and coercion until a person submits. Victims feel they must do what they are told; victims feel they are unable to leave and if they attempt to run, the people they love will be severely harmed. Traffickers are experts at breaking the will of their captives. After breaking the will of the victim, they groom the victim for upcoming acts with other abusers.

HUMAN TRAFFICKING DEFINED

Slavery is defined as 1: someone who is forced to work without pay, 2: a person who is strongly influenced and controlled by something, 3: completely subservient to a dominating influence. Human trafficking is the process where a person is enslaved. Slavery is the condition the person is in after he or she has been trafficked.

The U.S. Department of Health and Human Services defines human trafficking as "(a) sex trafficking in which a commercial sex act is induced by force, fraud, or coercion, or in which the person induced to perform such act has not attained 18 years of age; or

(b) the recruitment, harboring, transportation, provision, or obtaining of a person for labor or services through the use of force, fraud, or coercion for the purposes of subjection to involuntary servitude, peonage, debt bondage, or slavery."

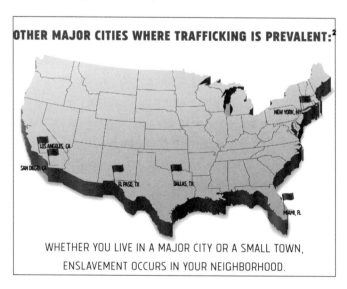

OTHER MAJOR CITIES WHERE TRAFFICKING IS PREVALENT:[2]

NEW YORK, NY

LOS ANGELES, CA

SAN DIEGO, CA

EL PASO, TX

DALLAS, TX

MIAMI, FL

WHETHER YOU LIVE IN A MAJOR CITY OR A SMALL TOWN, ENSLAVEMENT OCCURS IN YOUR NEIGHBORHOOD.

TRAFFICKING TAKES MANY FORMS

What does modern day slavery look like?

• In Nicaragua's capital city of Managua is a large dump. From far away, smoke is visible from the perpetual fires that burn the foul-smelling refuse. The residents that make their home at the dump generation after generation eke out subsistence by scrounging through the debris and reselling anything reusable. Trafficking in Managua looks like the mother that gives her daughter to the driver of the trash truck in exchange for first pick of whatever is in the truck.

• In China, trafficking looks like the children that are rounded up from the streets for being the three no-haves; no papers, no job, and no abode. Transported to work prisons, they are worked to death and die in obscurity. Some prisoners are executed and their organs harvested. Their fate remains a mystery to their families who never hear from them again.

• In California, trafficking looks like the child whose virginity was auctioned at a local bar by a drug-addicted mother. In South Carolina, trafficking looks like a shed behind an ethnic restaurant where victims are locked in until their shift to work off their transportation debt to their traffickers.

Human trafficking is divided into these categories:

FORCED LABOR

In January 2015, police raided three massage parlors in the upper class suburbs of Columbus, Ohio. Authorities rescued eighteen Chinese girls who were unpaid, unable to leave the parlors, and forced to sleep on the tables.

Also called involuntary servitude, forced labor results when dishonest employers exploit workers who may be vulnerable because of high rates of unemployment, poverty, crime, discrimination, corruption, political conflict, or a cultural acceptance of mistreatment. Immigrants are especially vulnerable, but people can be forced to labor in their own countries. Not all victims of sex trafficking are forced to labor, but female victims of forced or bonded labor and domestic servitude are often sexually exploited as well. Forced labor exists in agriculture, factories, domestic work, and when the laborer is unpaid.

ADULT SEX TRAFFICKING

An adult that is coerced, forced, deceived, or tricked into prostitution is a victim of trafficking. Those that recruit, transport, harbor, receive, or obtain a human being commit a trafficking crime as do those that use psychological manipulation or physical force to hold a person in service. A pimp – which is another term for trafficker – will threaten, manipulate, trick, blackmail, and hurt a girl or her family if she does not sell herself for sex. The trafficker keeps the money earned by the girl.

BONDED LABOR

In Honduras, two young men saw an advertisement offering a good salary for work at a hotel in the United States. They paid for their airfare, travel, and a fee to a job recruiter. When the optimistic young men arrived in Florida, they were forced into an apartment with 17 other people, taken to and from work each day, and only given a small portion of what they earned.

Bonded labor or debt bondage is the criminal practice of enslaving a person under the condition that the person owes and must repay a debt. Traffickers recruit workers from poor countries with the promise of good jobs and a good life in the United States. The hopeful workers are smuggled into the U.S. illegally and forced to work to pay off an impossible amount for their passage. Victims will never work off the debt because the traffickers have no intentions of ever letting them free. The victims are enslaved.

INVOLUNTARY DOMESTIC SERVITUDE

In 2012, two people in Detroit, Michigan were convicted of forced labor and slavery of minors. For five years, they deprived four youth from another country of food and sleep, and forced them to do domestic labor.

Involuntary domestic servitude occurs when someone is enslaved in a household setting to work as a maid, cook, nanny, or gardener. Involuntary servitude of domestic workers often results in isolation from anyone outside the household, untreated illness, and sexual abuse. Authorities cannot inspect private property as easily as formal workplaces.

FORCED CHILD LABOR

Child labor cases in the U.S. include a child forced to sell candy bars after school until the box was gone or the child was not allowed to return home or eat. Child labor occurs where young children work long hours without pay in family businesses, factories, or as migrant field workers. Homeless children panhandling for survival and forced to give the money to another person as depicted in the movie, *August Rush*, is forced child labor.

While children may legally engage in certain forms of work, forced child labor is the sale and trafficking of children and their entrapment in brutal bonded labor. Forced child labor happens anywhere a child cannot leave and is coerced to perform work that financially benefits someone outside the child's family.

CHILD SOLDIERS

Child soldiering involves the unlawful military use of children through force, fraud, or coercion to be combatants, laborers, or sexually exploited by armed forces. Government forces, paramilitary organizations, or rebel groups have been known to abduct children to be used as combatants, work as porters, cooks, guards, servants, messengers, or spies. Both male and female child soldiers are often sexually abused and are at high risk of contracting sexually transmitted diseases.

There are 14 countries where child soldiers continue to be a crime against children: Afghanistan, Burma, Central African Republic, Chad, Colombia, Democratic Republic of Congo, India, Philippines, Somalia, South Sudan, Sudan, Thailand, and Yemen.

CHILD BRIDES

Each year over 15 million girls are forced into marriage before they reach 18 years old or the legal age of adulthood. The highest rates of child brides are in Bangladesh, Central African Republic, Chad, Guinea, Mali, and Niger.

ORGAN TRAFFICKING

The demand worldwide for organ transplants supersedes the natural availability of important organs including heart, liver, and kidneys. Traffickers kidnap and murder people to harvest and sell the victim's organs on the black market.

INTERNATIONAL ADOPTIONS

Because the adoption process in the United States is difficult, expensive, and time-consuming, many people resort to adopting a child from another country. Through bribes, baby stealing, and buying babies from vulnerable people, traffickers corrupt the adoption system. Some countries implemented stricter laws and requirements to curtail the trafficking of babies.

CHILD SEX TRAFFICKING

The use of children in the commercial sex trade is prohibited worldwide yet continues to increase. Commercial sex is a sex act, which includes stripping or exotic dancing, pornography or escorting, exchanged for something of financial value. Sex trafficking has devastating consequences for minors, including long-lasting physical and psychological trauma, disease including HIV/AIDS, drug addiction, unintended pregnancy, malnutrition, social ostracism, and death.

Most at risk for child sex trafficking in the U.S. are youth who have been molested or abused, runaways, and children from impoverished communities. However, child sex trafficking can occur in any neighborhood and to any child.

SUMMARY

Illegal in every nation on the globe, modern day slavery is called human trafficking. Currently there are more slaves than at any other time in history including when slavery was legal. Slavery comes in many forms and looks like many different things.

FREEDOM FIGHTERS CHALLENGE

WHEN YOU ARE OUT AND ABOUT, ENGAGE OTHERS IN CONVERSATION ABOUT MODERN DAY SLAVERY. EDUCATE OTHERS THAT THIS IS HAPPENING ALL AROUND THEM.

CHAPTER TWO

WHO: PROFILE OF A VICTIM

IN THIS CHAPTER:
GROOMED
TRICKED
TRAPPED

> *You gain strength, courage, and confidence by every experience*
> *in which you really stop to look fear in the face.*
> *You are able to say to yourself, I lived through this horror.*
> *I can take the next thing that comes along.'*
> *You must do the thing you think you cannot do.*
> — *Eleanor Roosevelt*

BLONDE AND GREEN-EYED THERESA was the new kid in school. Her dad was a successful businessman, and promotions required the family to move every two years. When Theresa was 15 years old, her family came to live in the upscale community of Birmingham near

Detroit in Michigan. The students at her new school were wealthier and of many different ethnicities than the friends she knew in smaller Midwest towns where she had lived before. Feeling awkward and eager to fit in, she was flattered when an older, good-looking boy began to pay attention to her.

GROOMING:

TO TRAIN FOR A SPECIFIC POSITION. TRAFFICKERS BEFRIEND A VICTIM, AND SPEND MONTHS GETTING TO KNOW AND SHOWERING HER WITH GIFTS. THEY BUY HER EXPENSIVE CLOTHES, GIVE HER MONEY, GET HER NAILS DONE, BUY HER A CAR, AND MAKE HER FEEL SPECIAL. IN THE MOVIE, *BAIT AND SWITCH*, A PIMP DESCRIBED HOW HE FINDS GIRLS TO TRAFFICK, "I GO TO THE MALL AND LOOK FOR THE AVERAGE GIRL. I DON'T APPROACH THE PRETTIEST GIRL BECAUSE SHE USUALLY HAS HIGH SELF-ESTEEM AND I DON'T APPROACH THE UGLIEST GIRL BECAUSE SHE WOULDN'T BELIEVE ME. I GO FOR THE MIDDLE GIRL AND SAY, 'YOU HAVE PRETTY EYES.' IF SHE TAKES THE BAIT AND IS IMPRESSED, THEN I HAVE HER."

VICTIMS CAN BE GROOMED BY:

- JOB OFFERS THAT MAKE A LARGE AMOUNT OF MONEY FOR LITTLE WORK OR GLAMOUR JOBS LIKE MODELING OR ACTING
- EXPENSIVE ITEMS
- CELL PHONES
- DRUGS
- ANYTHING THAT SOUNDS TOO GOOD TO BE TRUE

Her parents did not permit Theresa to date until she was 16 years old. Yet when this boy asked if she wanted a ride home from school, Theresa didn't think of it as a date and eagerly said yes. Skipping track practice after school, she excitedly got into his shiny new car. But instead of turning out of the parking lot toward her home, he steered the opposite way.

"I just want to stop by my house to get something," the boy explained.

At his mansion, he invited Theresa to come inside. Knowing her parents would not approve she decided to wait in the car until he returned.

He leaned close. "I like you."

He goes to my school, we have classes together, and we attend the same church, so what could happen? Theresa talked herself out of her gut feelings – her intuition – that told her getting in his car and going into his house when her parents thought she was at sports practice were bad ideas. Inside he gave her a Coke that was laced with drugs. Then he raped her.

HELPFUL RULES:

CHILDREN MAY FEEL THAT THEIR PARENTS ARE TOO STRICT. AS IN THERESA'S CASE, YOUNG PEOPLE OFTEN BELIEVE THE RULES THEIR PARENTS ESTABLISH ARE UNFAIR. "MY PARENTS DON'T TRUST ME" IS A COMMON COMPLAINT. CHILDREN CAN FEEL OTHERS HAVE LESS RULES, GET TO DO MORE, AND HAVE BETTER POSSES- SIONS. MANY CHILDREN THINK THEIR PARENTS DON'T UNDERSTAND THEIR WORLD AND THEIR LIFE.

HOWEVER, PARENTS CARE DEEPLY AND MAKE RULES TO PRO- TECT CHILDREN FROM HARMFUL SITUATIONS LIKE THERESA EXPE- RIENCED. THESE TIPS MAY NOT SEEM COOL, BUT THEY COULD POTENTIALLY KEEP YOU ALIVE:

• LISTEN TO YOUR PARENT. PARENTS REALLY DO KNOW BEST AND HAVE A REASON FOR THEIR RULES.

• TRUST THAT YOUR PARENTS ARE PROTECTING YOU FROM BEING HURT IN WAYS YOU CAN'T IMAGINE.

• CALL HOME BEFORE YOU GET INTO A CAR EVEN WITH A FRIEND.

• SHARE WITH YOUR PARENT WHO YOU TALK WITH ON SOCIAL MEDIA AND TEXTING.

• HONESTLY TELL YOUR PARENT WHEN SOMETHING HAPPENS – EVEN IF EVENTS OCCURRED BECAUSE YOU DISOBEYED YOUR PAR- ENTS.

• NEVER KEEP A BULLY'S SECRETS. IF YOU ARE HURT OR THREATENED, TELL YOUR PARENT OR ANOTHER TRUSTED ADULT RIGHT AWAY.

TRICKED

The boy took Theresa home where she was too embarrassed and humiliated to tell her parents what had happened. A few days later back at school, the boy gave her a large envelope. Inside were photos of her from that day at his house. Except in the photos, no one could tell that these were images taken during a rape. Everyone knew she had a crush on him. No one would believe that she was not a willing participant in these photos.

"My cousins were at my house that day and took these pictures," the older boy said. "If you don't want them to show these photos to your dad, you have to work for them. If you don't, my cousins will give these pictures to your father's boss, the priest at our church, and post them all around school."

Shocked, Theresa quickly considered. These people had businesses in town and she imagined that she could work several times at the retail counter or clean the shop to earn back the harmful photos. No one would have to know her embarrassing and shameful secret.

That night the phone rang in her room.

"You have to come now," said the boy on the other end.

Theresa looked at the time. "It's midnight. I'll get in trouble. I'm not allowed out this late – "

"You have to," he replied. "Or my cousins will show the pictures. You know those photos will destroy your family. Meet me outside."

Quietly, so as not to wake her parents, Theresa slipped out of the house. Still in her pajamas and barefoot, she once again got into the older student's car. He took her to another large and beautiful house. Through a private entrance, he steered her into an elaborately decorated basement with a big screen TV, huge stereo system, oversized furniture, and many men that were waiting for her.

The older cousin who had taken the photos approached her. "You want to keep your sweet little puppy alive? Keep your brothers safe? Make sure nothing happens to your mother and father?"

She meekly nodded.

"Don't even think about telling anyone," he threatened. "Don't ever think about not obeying."

TRAPPED

That night Theresa's nightmare began. She wouldn't earn back the horrible pictures by working in a store or doing their schoolwork. Instead, she was sold to strangers for sex.

After long days at school and afternoons of homework, she dropped exhausted into bed. Around midnight the phone would ring. Not bothering to brush her hair, apply makeup, or change into clothes, she tiptoed barefoot to the door and outside.

Night after night Theresa experienced sexual abuse and torture until she passed out. The young teen never knew where she was taken, the address, or what part of town she was in. No one asked her name, age, or why she was there. She was raped by hundreds of cruel men, but no one ever asked if she needed help. She couldn't go home until they were finished with her. She was a slave.

The traffickers followed her younger brother, came to where she worked, and left dead animals in her mailbox. The message was clear: Do what we say or your family will be hurt.

Even though some of her traffickers were in high school, the adults in Theresa's life were as intimidated by them as she was. Teachers never questioned the times Theresa was pulled out of class but allowed her to go as if she had simply asked for a hall pass to use the restroom. Although she was frequently away from school, she never received a detention. Never received a reprimand for skipping class. No one cared that her grades dropped from A's to barely passing.

Theresa dreamed that one-day her typing teacher, math teacher, study hall monitor, the teacher whose class was near her locker, or the school's security guard would say, "Theresa, can I help you? Are you okay?" Though they saw her slammed against the locker, spit on, harassed, and almost daily leave with her abusers, no one ever asked, "Are they hurting you? Do you need to talk?"

Theresa's constant challenge was to protect her family. Attending one out of five track practices, she told the coach she had a job and couldn't always be there. She told her mom she was at track practice. Her mother didn't come to practice nor did the coach call her parents to verify that she had a job. Babysitting after school was another excuse. The adults in Theresa's life never requested the phone number where she was.

The physical abuse left marks. "Oh, that bruise?" Theresa would answer casually. "I got that from not making it over the hurdle at track practice."

"My brother hit me," she'd explain away another mark. Or, "I ran into something at work." Make-up covered bruises on her face. Clothing concealed marks on other areas of her body. Hats or different hairstyles camouflaged bald spots where her hair had been yanked.

HUMAN TRAFFICKING BY THE NUMBERS:[1]

- 0: THE NUMBER OF COUNTRIES WITH LEGALIZED SLAVERY
- 27 MILLION: THE NUMBER OF SLAVES AROUND THE WORLD
- 800,000: NUMBER OF PEOPLE TRAFFICKED ACROSS INTERNATIONAL BORDERS EACH YEAR
- $90: GLOBALLY THE AVERAGE COST OF A SLAVE
- $32 BILLION: THE AMOUNT OF PROFITS GENERATED BY THE HUMAN TRAFFICKING INDUSTRY
- $15.5 BILLION: AMOUNT OF MONEY GENERATED BY HUMAN TRAFFICKING IN INDUSTRIALIZED NATIONS
- $9.7 BILLION: MONEY MADE IN THE UNITED STATES THROUGH HUMAN TRAFFICKING
- 80%: NUMBER OF VICTIMS THAT ARE FEMALE
- 70%: NUMBER OF FEMALE VICTIMS TRAFFICKED FOR SEX

SUMMARY

Traffickers befriend lonely and vulnerable people by acting extra nice and offering something that is too good to be true. They groom victims and then trick them into a job or sex. Traffickers trap their victims so the victim feels that they cannot tell anyone.

FREEDOM FIGHTERS CHALLENGE

HAVE YOU HAD A STRANGE FEELING WHEN SOMEONE WAS EXTRA NICE TO YOU? WAS THERE A TIME WHEN THE ACTIONS AND BEHAVIOR OF ANOTHER PERSON FELT INAUTHENTIC? WHAT DID YOU DO? HAVE YOU BEEN IN A SITUATION WHERE YOU WERE SCARED? HOW DID YOU REACT? IF YOU WERE IN THERESA'S SITUATION, WHAT WOULD YOU DO?

CHAPTER THREE

TARGETING CHILDREN

IN THIS CHAPTER:

WHO IS VULNERABLE?

300,000 AMERICAN CHILDREN

1.3 MILLION MISSING AND RUNAWAY CHILDREN

*There can be no keener revelation of a society's soul than
the way in which it treats its children.*
— *Nelslon Mandela*

WHEN YOUNG PEOPLE ARE ISOLATED from healthy relationships, they become vulnerable to people with evil intent. And while different groups are more vulnerable than others, traffickers aren't prejudiced in who they prey upon.

VULNERABLE: BOYS

For Joel, confiding in a friend changed his life. Joel's parents were divorced. Living with his drug-addicted dad was not conducive to doing well in school. But Joel's mom barely made ends meet and there often was not enough food at her house. Joel shared his situation with a friend on his high school sports team. The friend's parents asked Joel's mom if Joel could live with their family while Joel finished high school. Joel would have a safe and solid home close enough to see his mom and have holidays together. Everyone agreed this would be beneficial for Joel who promised to keep up his grades and help with chores at his friend's house while he lived there.

Boys who are trafficked are often forced into some of the following activities:

• pick fruit and vegetables, harvest grain, or slaughter animals
• sew carpets or stitch clothing
• make bricks
• make athletic equipment, fashion household goods or assemble toys
• sell candy bars or magazines door to door

More common in third world nations, thousands of enslaved children die each year when they must untangle fishing nets in deep and cold water, dive to harvest a quota of pearls or prawns (shrimp). In Thailand, where slavery is illegal, thousands of boys and men are tortured to harvest without pay much of the shrimp we eat in America. Stores like Wal-Mart, Tesco, Carrefour, and Costco purchase these items from slave dealers to sell cheaply to the consumer. In the Ivory Coast of Africa, young boys who have been kidnapped and beaten collect cocoa beans that are then purchased by companies like Hershey and Nestle to be made into cocoa products that are sold to American consumers.

Half the world's child soldiers are located in Africa. Rebels kill several children while their playmates watch. Then through violence, brainwashing, and drugs, the children are trained to use guns and machetes, and forced into military combat.

Those that traffick human organs trick, convince, and force victims to surrender lungs and kidneys for transplants. Some children are killed and their bodies are pieced out.

VULNERABLE: GIRLS

After two horrific years of torture and abuse, Theresa was relieved to learn that her family was moving to another state far away from the suburb of Detroit. Far away from her traffickers. When Theresa first learned the news, she carefully kept quiet about the upcoming relocation. If they knew, her traffickers would take her one night and never return Theresa to her home again. Her parents would never know what happened to their daughter and Theresa's fate would be like most victims of trafficking. She would be used until she was killed. Because Theresa was able to keep the secret of her family's upcoming move just like she had guarded the secret of her brutal abuse, Theresa is one of the rare survivors of human trafficking.

Most trafficked victims don't live to tell about it. Just before the move that saved her life, Theresa noticed the boy who had taken her to his house and raped her was paying attention to another girl. Like Theresa, Janie was shy and lonely. Her parents were divorced, her dad wasn't around to protect his daughter, and her mother was exhausted from working hard to pay the mortgage and keep food in the cupboard. Theresa knew the traffickers were grooming this girl in the same way they had groomed her and Theresa cared too much to let another teen get hurt. Though no one had helped Theresa, she desperately wanted to protect her schoolmate.

One day after school Theresa walked home with Janie. The girl kept looking over her shoulder. At Janie's house, the girls ate junk food and listened to music. Theresa asked, "Are you dating anyone? I saw you with a guy last week?"

Janie was defensive. "So what if I am?"

"Please be careful!" Theresa pleaded, "You don't know what you're getting yourself into. He is very dangerous."

"You're wrong, Theresa," Janie argued. "He loves me. He wouldn't hurt me. He told me."

"Janie, these guys will make you do things you don't want to. They will hurt you – "

Janie stood. "You should go, Theresa. They warned me that you might try to convince me not to go out with him. That you would say things to me. I am not even supposed to talk to you."

Theresa groaned. "They will suck you in. They will hold something over your head so you – "

Janie opened the door. "Good-bye, Theresa."

Longing to keep Janie from her same fate, Theresa telephoned many times and tried to talk to Janie in class. She wrote notes during school but Janie wouldn't read them. Knowing too well what was happening, Theresa was sickened to watch Janie get into the older boy's car after school just as Theresa had done on that fateful day that changed her life forever. As the weeks progressed, Janie's spirit shriveled and died. Theresa's nightmare had become hers.

Years later Theresa traveled back to Birmingham and spoke about human trafficking in the same city where she had been trafficked. Theresa wept bitterly as she drove along the highway and recognized areas where she had been taken as a young teen. Theresa also tried unsuccessfully to locate Janie. Perhaps the girl married and changed her name. Or moved far away like Theresa did.

More likely, Janie didn't survive the ordeal she most surely faced after Theresa escaped. Years later, Theresa saw an article in the Detroit newspaper about an upper class, white girl in her early twenties who had disappeared and was later found murdered. There were rumors that she had been secretly dating an older man. Theresa thought again of Janie and wondered how many girls were victimized in this way. The appetites of these evil men were unquenchable.

Up to 80 percent of trafficked victims are girls but they don't necessarily come from unhappy homes. They can come from upper class neighborhoods, two parent families with influential family members, have loving parents, or be cheerleaders. Traffickers target middle school girls at the malls, libraries, movie theaters, and on social media.

HUMAN TRAFFICKING AROUND THE WORLD:[1]

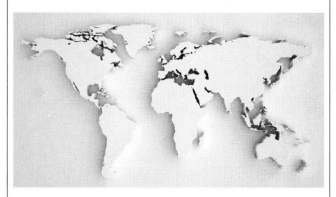

IMAGINE BEING A CHILD WHO IS TAKEN TO A FOREIGN PLACE ON THE OPPOSITE SIDE OF THE GLOBE WHERE YOU DON'T KNOW THE LANGUAGE, FOOD, CULTURE, OR THE PEOPLE. THAT IS WHAT HAPPENS TO CHILDREN TRAFFICKED INTO THE UNITED STATES FROM THE FOLLOWING PACIFIC ASIAN COUNTRIES:

- BURMA
- CAMBODIA
- CHINA
- INDONESIA
- JAPAN
- NORTH KOREA
- PHILIPPINES
- SINGAPORE
- SOUTH KOREA
- TAIWAN
- THAILAND
- VIETNAM

FIND THESE COUNTRIES ON A MAP AND SEE HOW FAR CHILDREN ARE TAKEN FROM THEIR HOME AND ALL THAT IS FAMILIAR TO THEM. THE UNITED STATES MAY SEEM FAMILIAR AND SAFE TO US, BUT HOW WOULD IT FEEL TO A TEN-YEAR-OLD WHO IS FAR FROM HOME AND CANNOT READ, WRITE, OR SPEAK ENGLISH?

MISSING CHILDREN AND RUNAWAYS

There are 1.3 million missing and runaway youth in the United States. Nearly 3,500 go missing every day. Teens run away from home because they:

- are abused
- may be molested
- are neglected
- don't feel loved

Youth that leave home are susceptible to becoming trafficked. The chances are very high that within 48 hours, a pimp will approach a teen and offer protection, food, shelter, and money. One in six runaways are trafficked, sold to strangers for sex. Cross-country stings resulted in the rescue of youth as young as nine years old from prostitution rings.

The National Center for Missing and Exploited Children (www.missingkids.com) create posters featuring children who have been reported missing. These posters report the child's age, weight, height, where they are from, and when they went missing. Additional information such as tattoos, piercing, what they were last seen wearing, where they may be headed, or who they were last seen with is included with a phone number to call if you recognize the person (1-800-The Lost).

Human trafficking enslaves nearly 13 million children as victims of forced labor, bonded labor, and forced prostitution. Congressional findings report that in the United States alone, every year an estimated 100,000 to 300,000 American children are sexually exploited. Human trafficking happens in every community in America.

WHO WILL HELP?

Theresa dreamed, wished, and prayed for a person to help. For someone to see the truth. For God to send someone to rescue her.

For Theresa, that person never showed up. Not:
- the guidance counselor who failed to ask why her grades were falling
- the principal who didn't ask why she skipped class
- the security guard in the school hallway who ignored the physical abuse she endured
- the teachers who turned their back when she was harassed
- the policeman who took her home after she was kidnapped, drugged, and left for dead
- her boyfriend who knew something was amiss
- fellow students who knew she was bullied
- her parents who didn't question where she was, how she looked, or the change in her bright personality

No one cared enough to protect a teen that was being victimized. Enslaved. Trafficked. No one wanted to get involved.

Like Theresa, a child is exploited somewhere in the world every 26 seconds. How would you respond if Theresa had been that girl?

- in your classroom
- on your school bus
- in your lunch room
- on your sports team
- worked at the same job
- who attended your church
- was in your youth group
- belonged to the same club
- was in your school band

DECREASING VULNERABILITY:

"MY PARENTS DON'T CARE." YOUNG PEOPLE MAY FEEL LIKE THEIR PARENTS DON'T CARE. USUALLY PARENTS CARE DEEPLY. BUT THERE ARE OCCASIONS WHEN A PARENT IS ABSENT OR DRUG ADDICTED OR IS INVOLVED IN OTHER SERIOUS ISSUES THAT INTERFERE WITH BEING A WISE AND CONCERNED PARENT. IF THAT IS THE CASE:

- GET INVOLVED WITH STRONG ADULTS THROUGH SCHOOL, FRIENDS, CHURCH, AND YOUTH GROUPS.
- ESTABLISH PROTECTIVE GUIDELINES FOR YOURSELF SUCH AS STAY IN SCHOOL, GET GOOD GRADES, AND DON'T TAKE RIDES FROM PEOPLE UNLESS SOMEONE WHO CARES ABOUT YOU APPROVES.
- GET INVOLVED IN REGULAR PROGRAMS WHERE YOU HAVE CONSISTENT ACCOUNTABILITY LIKE FAITH-BASED ACTIVITIES, SPORTS, CLUBS, OR MUSIC.

- DO YOU HAVE RELATIVES YOU WOULD BE SAFE TO LIVE WITH?

- TELL A COUNSELOR AT SCHOOL ABOUT YOUR SITUATION AND LET THEM HELP YOU SET A PLAN TO KEEP YOU SAFE.

- TALK TO A SCHOOL COUNSELOR, FAVORITE TEACHER, COACH, YOUTH LEADER, OR FRIEND'S PARENTS ABOUT YOUR SITUATION.

SUMMARY

Thirteen million children are trafficked worldwide. Human trafficking occurs in nearly every city in the nation. In the United States, traffickers exploit up to 300,000 children every year. Many victims don't feel as if they can tell anyone or escape. Missing children and runaways are the most vulnerable.

FREEDOM FIGHTERS CHALLENGE

IDENTIFY WAYS THAT YOU ARE VULNERABLE.

- WHAT WOULD YOU DO IF SOMEONE HAD EMBARRASSING OR HUMILIATING PHOTOS OF YOU? THREATENED YOUR FAMILY?

- DO YOU HAVE FRIENDS OR A SIBLING WHO ARE VULNERABLE?

- WHAT WOULD YOU HAVE DONE DIFFERENTLY THAN THERESA IF THIS HAPPENED TO YOU?

- IF YOU SUSPECT SOMEONE IS BEING BULLIED AND HARMED, WOULD YOU MAKE THE BRAVE CHOICE TO ACT ON YOUR CONCERNS WITH HOPES OF SAVING A PERSON?

- WOULD YOU IGNORE IT? WISH IT AWAY? TURN YOUR BACK?

CHAPTER FOUR

WHAT A TRAFFICKER DOESN'T WANT YOU TO KNOW

IN THIS CHAPTER:
PROFILE OF A TRAFFICKER
TYPES OF TRAFFICKERS
PIMP OR TRAFFICKER?
TRAFFICK VICTIM OR PROSTITUTE?

> *Those who enslave other peoples enslave themselves.*
> — *Herbert Spencer*

ONE DAY, THE BOY DROVE THERESA back to the place where she was first raped and where her slavery began. Today the driveway was filled with cars and she shut her eyes against the growing feeling of doom.

Downstairs, the boy led her to the bedroom. The second bedroom door was open. That was unusual because it was always closed. Theresa tried to peek in to see the man she had heard about. He seemed to be the one in charge. Sometimes she heard him outside the room barking orders at the other men who either revered or feared him. Once she asked about him and was slapped across the face.

"Never mention him again," she was told as she rubbed her stinging cheek. "He doesn't exist. For your own good, don't ever say his name. Understood?"

Today, a deep, older voice came from the other bedroom. "Bring her in here."

The outer room was suddenly quiet when they realized she was being summoned to *him*.

"Now!" he boomed.

Theresa was pushed into the room that was lavishly decorated with oversized wooden furniture and expensive, richly colored fabrics.

Lounging comfortably upon his massive bed was a man in his late twenties. "I can make your life very easy or very hard. Do you know that?"

"How much harder can it be?" *Much worse and Theresa knew she would be dead.*

Slowly he looked Theresa over. "They treated you very hard today, didn't they?"

Tears filled Theresa's eyes.

"I can take all that away. I can give you a very nice life. I can stop all the pain. Would you like that?"

She didn't know what to say.

"They will continue to hurt you and I will give them permission to do whatever they want to you. Or you can work solely for me. If you don't, I can't promise what will happen." He continued, "I can make your life easier. You'll have your own nice apartment, designer clothes, and all the money you could ask for."

His offer was to keep Theresa as his prostitute for wealthier, more powerful men. The head of a mafia, this man intimidated and terrorized. He embodied power and control and money. Theresa had no idea what to expect but knew his plans meant one night she would be taken away. Given a new name, new identity, new clothing, and a new environment, she would be forced to run away, and be at someone's complete will, never knowing what was going to happen. Her dreams for college and a normal life would die. Driven to an apartment in a strange part of town, she would be locked away and never see her family again.

PROFILE OF A TRAFFICKER

Why would someone choose to enslave a fellow human being? Also called pimps, traffickers use violence and psychological manipulation to control people and convert their bodies into cash. It is compelled service. How does someone become a pimp/trafficker and what drives their ability to abuse innocent people? Do these controlling bullies have vulnerabilities?

Lacking *empathy – the ability to understand and sympathize with how another feels* – a trafficker's cold personality is the largest contributor to selling others as an entrepreneurial venture. Some pimps and traffickers had family members such as parents, siblings, and other relatives who engaged in commercial sex either as facilitators or sex workers. Many grew up in neighborhoods where prostitution was a common part of everyday life. Individuals engaged in illegal activities including drug dealing frequently work as pimps.

Drug dealers are moving into human trafficking because when they sell their drugs, they have to get more. But they can sell a person over and over again. These criminals don't value women as humans but view females only as commodities. Drug dealers typically get more prison time and are more easily apprehended than human traffickers.

In the United States, traffickers typically fall into three networks:

- Asian
- Latino
- Domestic

Serving mostly Asian clientele and generally run by Asian men and older Asian women, Asian networks deal mostly with South Korean, Chinese, and Thai girls and children. Controlled by Latino men from places ranging from Mexico to South America, Latino traffickers often target girls from the same countries as the men that enslave them. Thugs from the United States run domestic traffick rings that sell American girls into the sex trade. All three networks use complex transportation methods to control the girls they take to clients. Domestic traffickers use their own vehicles to transport their victims.

 COMPELLED SERVICE *n.* com·pelled ser·vice \kəm-'peld\ \'sər-vəs\ **1.** BEING, OR FEELING, FORCED TO DO SOMETHING.

Traffickers come in many forms:
- Organized criminal rings
- Pimps (Gorilla, Romeo, and Popcorn)
- Family members
- Employers
- Women

All traffickers use physical and emotional pressure to control those who are vulnerable. Traffickers are criminals and do intense prison time when caught and found guilty.

PIMP OR TRAFFICKER?

A pimp is always a trafficker but a trafficker is not always a pimp. When is a trafficker not a pimp? Pimps sell sex. A trafficker that supplies human beings for labor, organs, child soldiers, or adoptions is trafficking in persons but not necessarily selling sex.

Traffickers use others for their own purposes. Primarily, traffickers use victims for money. Molesters, traffickers, and evil people are astute at preying upon a person's weaknesses. Void of a moral or ethical compass, they bully, threaten, manipulate, and hurt their victims after promising what the victim most wants. Some scenarios might include:

- Those in poverty — traffickers promise fast wealth in exchange for a kidney.
- The poor — exploiters offer a dream job and a hopeful future.
- The hungry — an abuser dangles the opportunity to have food in abundance.
- The lonely — the false assurance of relationship.
- The unloved — starved, naïve, and trusting. Bullies bait with gifts and sweet talk.

It seems too good to be true. And it is. The trap is set and sprung. Like Theresa and Janie, the victims' lives are stolen.

PSYCHOLOGICAL MANIPULATORS

To gain control over their victims, pimps use psychological manipulation including:

- conceal aggressive intentions and actions
- know the victim's mental and emotional vulnerabilities
- ruthlessly cause harm to others to achieve own desires (threaten to hurt family members)
- seclude or isolate the victim from others
- brain wash and tell the victim lies
- manipulation

PSYCHOLOGICAL MANIPULATION *n.*
psy·cho·log·i·cal ma·nip·u·la·tion
\ˌsī-kə-ˈlä-ji-kəl\ \mə-ˈni-pyə-ˌlā-shun\

1. A PROCESS BY WHICH A PERSON USES DECEPTIVE, UNDERHANDED, AND ABUSIVE METHODS TO CHANGE THE PERCEPTION OR BEHAVIOR OF OTHERS. THROUGH ABUSE, EXPLOITATION, DECEPTION, AND DEVIOUSNESS, MANIPULATORS USE OTHERS TO GET THEIR OWN WAY.

Psychological manipulators are adept at targeting people who are:

- addicted to earning the approval and acceptance of others – often called people pleasers
- fearful of expressing negative emotions including anger, frustration, or disapproval
- lacking in the ability to say no

- highly dependent on others
- not self-reliant
- naïve – refusing to believe some people are ruthless
- without confidence, have low self-esteem
- willing to accept blame
- emotionally dependent
- believe the manipulator has an understandable reason to be hurtful
- inexperienced
- lonely or shy
- marginalized
- starved for attention from men and desperate to be loved

MANIPULATION ELICITS ANGER

WHEN YOU FEEL LIKE YOU ARE BEING MANIPULATED, IT IS NATURAL TO FEEL ANGRY. THOSE WHO ARE INEXPERIENCED IN DEALING WITH THEIR OWN FEELINGS CAN BE UNCOMFORTABLE WITH THEIR ANGER. BEING DEFENSIVE AND JUSTIFYING YOUR ANGER TO THE PERSON MANIPULATING YOU IS A SIGN THAT YOU ARE TAKING RESPONSIBILITY FOR SOMEONE ELSE'S ACTIONS. "YOU MADE ME (ANGRY, HIT YOU, HURT YOU)" ARE WRONG STATEMENTS. COERCION AND MANIPULATION ARE ALWAYS WRONG. THE ANGER A PERSON FEELS WHEN HE OR SHE IS MANIPULATED IS THE EXTRA ADRENALIN NEEDED TO RIGHT A WRONG. EACH PERSON IS PERSONALLY RESPONSIBLE FOR HIS OR HER OWN ACTIONS, BEHAVIOR, AND EMOTIONS.

GORILLA PIMP

Occasionally traffickers are violent from the first contact with a victim. This is called a gorilla pimp; someone who is heavy handed, uses force, and at times kidnapping. The pimp is usually someone the victim knows and initially he may be a smooth talker, protective, or a type of father figure. But a gorilla pimp soon resorts to violence to force the victim to do what he wants.

ROMEO PIMP

The majority of girls forced into prostitution in the United States are American citizens. Initially many victims don't realize they have a pimp. A Romeo pimp is a handsome man who is smooth talking, charming, and pretends to be the girl's boyfriend. He is romantically involved with her and may be her age or much older. He tells her she is beautiful and gives her compliments. Though he may not look like the stereotype, any person who receives money for her is her pimp.

POPCORN PIMP

A popcorn pimp is considered the lowest type of pimp. He typically does drugs and has only one or two girls working for him.

Pimps also go by the names: Mack, Hustler, and Player.

FAMILY MEMBERS

In the U.S., 32 percent of human trafficking victims were initially trafficked by a family member. Victims may be sold by:

- a brother to friends to supply a drug habit
- an older sister whose husband threatened her
- a grandparent to the landlord in exchange for rent
- abusive parents greedy for money

WOMEN

Most traffickers or pimps are male. However, the number of women who are becoming traffickers is growing. Female pimps, called madams, befriend girls and convince them that sex is a way to make a lot of money. But quickly the madam becomes very violent, controls the girl, and keeps the money. Many female traffickers were once trafficking victims themselves. The victim is deceived because females expect to trust one another.

EMPLOYER

Based on the demands of their clientele, traffickers ensnare American children. Of the estimated 17,500 people trafficked into the United States each year, half are children. The majority of victims brought as slaves to the United States come from the Pacific/East Asia.

- 50% will be prostituted
- 27% will be used in domestic servitude
- 10% percent in agricultural work
- 5% percent as factory workers

Pimps and traffickers focus on how much money customers – called *johns* – are willing to pay to exploit victims. Do their johns prefer Asian females, Latino, or American girls? Are their customers looking for domestic help, labor, or girls to be available for a group of businessmen?

Any time large numbers of people congregate, traffickers are near to do business. When the Super Bowl was held in New Orleans, Theresa and another survivor were there to rescue victims. On Bourbon Street, Toshia noticed a suspicious man.

She asked him, "Are you a pimp?"

He laughed and said, "No. I am a facilitator of a good time! I am an entrepreneur."

PROSTITUTE OR TRAFFICK VICTIM?

There is no such thing as a child or teen prostitute. It is not natural for a child to know about or be involved with pimps and johns. Children dream about becoming an astronaut, nurse, teacher, or president, but no child imagines herself as a prostitute sold by a pimp to lustful men. By federal definition, if a person is under the age of 18 and involved in any form of commercial sex, she is being trafficked. Boys are also prostituted and usually by older men.

If a woman 18 years of age or older has a pimp, then she is being trafficked. He manipulates, threatens, controls, and sells her. It is illegal to sell another person. Pimps force women to work in strip clubs, brothels, escort services, or massage parlors. In June 2011, police raided a strip club in Akron, Ohio and found a 14-year-old girl employed as an erotic dancer. Her father had gotten the job for his daughter, made her work there, and took the money she earned.

Anyone who forces another to have sex and receives money for it is a pimp.

- A boyfriend that convinces a girl to have sex because he needs money is a pimp.
- A parent who sells a child is a pimp.
- The schoolmate who blackmailed Theresa is a pimp.
- The trafficker who kidnaps a girl and forces her to have sex at truck stops is a pimp.

SUMMARY

Void of empathy and compassion, a trafficker ruthlessly manipulates vulnerable and weaker people for their own financial gain. A trafficker can be another youth, a family member, employer, or stranger. Traffickers deceive victims by enticing and gaining trust. They use physical and psychological threats to victimize humans.

FREEDOM FIGHTERS CHALLENGE

VOID OF A MORAL COMPASS, TRAFFICKERS USE THREATS, MANIPULATION, COERCION, AND CRUELTY TO ENSNARE AND ENSLAVE VICTIMS. TALK TO YOUR FRIENDS ABOUT WHAT IS A MORAL COMPASS. WHAT IS YOUR MORAL COMPASS?

CHAPTER FIVE

PROFILE OF A JOHN

IN THIS CHAPTER:
USERS AND TAKERS
PORNOGRAPHY
SUPPLY AND DEMAND
THE SOLUTION

Human beings have within them the ability to choose evil or good.
— Adam Hamilton

DURING THE YEARS THERESA was delivered to new addresses and different men, no one asked why this young girl was not safely at home with her family getting a good night's rest before school the following day. Though Theresa was clearly not an adult, no one asked how old she was, who she was, or if she needed help. Living in Michigan, she was a slave.

USERS AND TAKERS

Someone that uses others and takes what isn't theirs is the definition of a john. People that pay to have sex are called johns. Selfish people, johns do not care about the victims they pay to violate.

In the United States it is illegal to buy or sell sex. Prostitution is not legal in the entirety of any state. There are 300,000 counties in the nation, and prostitution is legal in only eight counties. These counties are in Nevada, but Clark County, which contains Las Vegas, is not one of them. Although sex for sale is heavily advertised in Las Vegas, it is not legal there. The advertisements such as this are permitted under the freedom of speech right.

Johns come from every socioeconomic group in America. Most are:
- educated
- financially able to pay a trafficker
- husbands
- professional businessmen
- fathers with children of their own

A john steals the life of another human being. If the victim survives the abuses, the violence a john perpetrates on a fellow human leaves lifelong scars.

Johns are:
- the cause of sex trafficking
- the key to eradicating human trafficking

> **SOCIO-ECONOMICS** *n.* so·ci·o·ec·o·no·mics
> \sō–sē–ō–e–kə–'nä–miks\
>
> 1. THE STUDY OF HOW ECONOMIC SCIENCE AFFECTS AND INFLUENCES SOCIAL PHILOSOPHY, ETHICS, AND HUMAN DIGNITY. ECONOMICS HELPS PEOPLE UNDERSTAND THE PROCESS THAT GOVERNS PRODUCTION, DISTRIBUTION, AND CONSUMPTION OF GOODS AND SERVICES IN A CULTURE.

While it is not always possible to change a selfish person into someone respectful of others, society can stop sex trafficking by making the penalty for using a human trafficking victim so severe that the users no longer consider the prospect worthwhile.

Suggested penalties for johns include the following:
- charge with kidnapping, rape, and assault
- publish their name in their local newspaper
- give johns a special colored license plate indicating their offense
- list the john as a sex offender
- make them pay huge fines and increase jail time

Those in their community are often surprised to discover professionals that they believed were compassionate business people are secretly using people who are enslaved against their will.

According to research by Dr. Earl Henslin, a specialist who studies brain imaging, johns who victimize others for sex are addicted to pornography.

Their addiction to pornography fuels a depraved desire to use a sexual slave.

PORNOGRAPHY

Pornography is the portrayal of sexual subject matter for the purpose of sexual arousal. Viewing pornography launches chemicals in the brain that are as addictive as crack to a drug addict. The human brain is neuroplastic, meaning it works by changing its structure in response to repeated mental experience. Quickly, a damaged dopamine system demands sexual experiences that include harming others. Johns act out their addictions on real people – traffick victims like Theresa.

Pornographic images are now common. Explicit images are most common on the Internet as well as in the following:

- advertising
- television programming
- feature films
- song lyrics
- music videos

Seeing inappropriate images sends a message to the brain, and the body reacts with excitement and pleasure. But the next time the same picture is viewed the effect is nothing like it was before. The brain craves something stronger to once again react and becomes accustomed to inappropriate images that dishonor others. Pornography is suddenly normal to the brain and the body no longer reacts to it. A person, generally males but some females too, becomes addicted and seeks more graphic and demeaning content to trigger his or her body's reaction.

From images, the porn addict moves to watching pornographic movies. The addiction progresses quickly and soon the brain no longer responds to action films. The addict shifts to real people and frequents strip clubs or buys sex from women to reach that level of excitement. When the brain and body adjust to this level, the addict seeks alternatives to achieve that thrill. The porn addict eventually becomes a user – a john – and buys and violates victims.

SUPPLY AND DEMAND

Years ago a company in Kentucky did a profitable business making porch spindles, stair railings, and butter churns. A fan of a new game called baseball, the

FACTS ABOUT PORNOGRAPHY:

- PORNOGRAPHY IS ADDICTIVE.
- PORN IS COMMONLY AVAILABLE TO ALL AGES.

- PORNOGRAPHY IS A $13 BILLION INDUSTRY IN THE U.S.
- CHILD PORNOGRAPHY IS ILLEGAL IN MOST COUNTRIES.
- PORNOGRAPHY CONTRIBUTES TO VIOLENCE AGAINST FEMALES IN ITS PRODUCTION AND CONSUMPTION.
- MORE THAN 70 PERCENT OF MALE INTERNET USERS BETWEEN THE AGES OF 18 AND 34 VISIT A PORN SITE MONTHLY.
- PORNOGRAPHY REINFORCES MYTHS THAT WOMEN ENJOY BEING TREATED VIOLENTLY.
- PORN CAN DESTROY A MAN'S RELATIONSHIP TO HIS SPOUSE OR GIRLFRIEND RESULTING IN ADDITIONAL PORN USE.
- STATES WITH HIGH PORN USAGE ALSO HAVE HIGH DIVORCE RATES.
- PORN USAGE IS A CONTRIBUTING FACTOR IN CASES OF RAPE, DOMESTIC VIOLENCE, AND CHILD ABUSE.
- THE UNITED STATES IS THE HIGHEST CONSUMER OF PORNOGRAPHY.
- THE AVERAGE AGE WHEN AN AMERICAN FIRST VIEWS PORNOGRAPHY IS 11.
- SEXTING CAN BE A FORM OF CHILD PORNOGRAPHY.

owner's son convinced his father to tool an area of the factory to manufacture wooden bats. One day, grocery stores began to sell butter and housewives nationwide stopped using the time-consuming and labor-intensive butter churns in favor of purchasing pats of butter. Overnight, butter churns were no longer in demand. No longer was it profitable to continue to supply the now obsolete household butter maker because there was no more demand for that item.

However, baseball was rapidly becoming the national sport and the demand for wooden bats continued to escalate. The manufacturing company stopped making butter churns and retooled to meet the new demand. The favorite of baseball legends Babe Ruth, Ty Cobb, and Lou Gehrig, by 1923, Louisville Slugger was selling more bats than any other bat maker. The Louisville Slugger is an example of the law of supply and demand.

Modern day slavery would likely end if:

• no one forced another to labor without fair and compassionate compensation

• no men came night after night to violate young girls like Theresa

• the penalty for buying sex was so high, it was no longer worth it to those who do

When men no longer pay for girls, girls will no longer be victimized. Human trafficking exists based on economics. Business-minded people recognize or create a demand and then provide the supply. The principle of supply and demand is natural.

• People need food, so farmers provide crops.

• People like to be mobile, so manufacturers build cars.

• People participate in athletics, so companies

make soccer balls and baseball bats.

• Johns have an insatiable desire to harm victims, so traffickers provide slaves.

Unlimited by socioeconomic factors, human trafficking is driven by supply and demand. People, especially children, are a commodity in a multi-billion dollar industry that trades in human flesh. The industry is fueled first by:

• selfishness
• greed

Traffickers are the users and johns are the takers. Traffickers recognize that a large number of consumers will pay a great deal of money to satisfy their perverted desires. Sadly, the principle of supply and demand as it applies to human trafficking reflects an evil side of mankind.

Together, the users and the takers – traffickers and johns – victimize two children every minute.

• Warlords force children to be soldiers.
• Babies are sold for adoption.
• Those who are ill find replacement organs through the black market.
• People selfishly abuse those who are vulnerable.
• Labor traffickers value profits more highly than human dignity.

• In exchange for money, traffickers rob and sell human flesh.

SUMMARY

Without johns, human trafficking would no longer be lucrative.

FREEDOM FIGHTERS CHALLENGE

ALTHOUGH PORNOGRAPHY IS COMMONLY AVAILABLE, IT IS DANGEROUSLY ADDICTIVE AND CHANGES THE BRAIN AND PERSONALITY OF THE USER. WHAT CAN YOU DO TO PROTECT YOUR LIFE FROM PORNOGRAPHY? HOW CAN YOU PROTECT YOUR FAMILY AND COMMUNITY FROM THE DESTRUCTIVE EFFECTS OF PORNOGRAPHY?

CHAPTER SIX

HOW DOES TRAFFICKING FLOURISH?

IN THIS CHAPTER:
AGE OF ENTRY
MOST HIDDEN FORM OF ABUSE
COERCION AND THREATS

> *Just because we have a smile on our faces,*
> *doesn't mean we want to be there.*
> *— Traffick victim forced to work in a strip club*

VIOLENTLY FORCED INTO THE SEX TRADE, one young girl ultimately accepted her role and tried to attract buyers. Arrested several times for prostitution, the girl's arrest record was a tragic timeline of photos depicting a child being abused. Law enforcement officials did not recognize the signs of trafficking and each time she was released back into her life as a trafficking victim. Why would a girl go along with her abuse?

Professionals in the field of torture, domestic violence, child abuse, and commercial sexual exploitation refer to this process as seasoning, grooming, and/or conditioning. Abusers use isolation, induced debility, exhaustion, threats, degradation, enforcing of trivial demands, the granting of occasional indulgences, and physical torture to subjugate others to their demands.

SUBJUGATE v. sub·ju·gate \'səb-ji-ˌgāt\

1. TO DEFEAT AND GAIN CONTROL OVER ANOTHER THROUGH VIOLENCE. THE RESULT IS ILLUSTRATED IN THE PICTURE OF OXEN THAT IS OBEDIENT UNDER THE YOKE.

AGE OF ENTRY

A girl seen on a street corner may give the appearance of choosing to be in that place because the unseen forces that condition her to be there are as real as if they were yards of barbed wire. If a girl in Cambodia can be conditioned into prostitution, why can't an American girl?

A casual observer is unaware of the conditioning forced on a female until she accepts her fate. To the casual observer, it would appear that for two years Theresa willingly got into her trafficker's car. Those around Theresa did not understand that each time she ignored the telephone when it rang at night, a dead animal or a black rose was left in her mailbox. Theresa's dog was killed, and then a car followed her brother as he walked home from school and parked outside her house for hours. The warning was clear and it was deadly.

Consider human trafficking from a victim's perspective. No child's desired career choice is to be a prostitute, stripper, or work as a forced laborer. Prostitution and forced labor is human trafficking. Human trafficking has many faces and all of them are evil. The victim is a child. A child that *feels* there are no options.

People that are trafficked for labor range in age from the very young to the elderly. A U.S. Department of Health and Human Services found that the average age of entry as a female victim of sex trafficking is 12-14 years old and has been trending younger in recent years. The average age for boys is 11-13 years old.

Tens of thousands of American, Mexican, and Canadian youth become victims of juvenile pornography, prostitution, and trafficking every year. Researchers confirm that underage girls are the bulk – 80 percent – of the victims exploited in the commercial sex market that includes pornography, stripping, escort services, and prostitution. National stings have recovered trafficked children as young as eight years old from prostitution rings.

MOST HIDDEN FORM OF ABUSE

Traffickers target youth because children are far easier to deceive, threaten, coerce, force, manipulate, and blackmail. Due to their natural innocence, immaturity, and limited experience, young people are easily convinced that they do not have options or a choice.

Adults are designed to nurture and protect younger generations. Children are confused when those who should be trustworthy harm them instead of providing protection and nurture. Adults are deeply betrayed when fellow humans deceive them and steal their freedom.

The majority of children at risk of being trafficked are youth from:
- broken or single parent homes
- abusive and dysfunctional families
- the foster family system
- the streets because they are runaways

- children living in poverty
- homes where drugs are used

Exploitation of children is not limited to a particular racial, ethnic, or socioeconomic group. Many victimized children – like Theresa – live in secure, middle class homes, and few parents are aware of their child's involvement in pornography and prostitution.

Theresa was in the rare 20 percent of trafficking victims that didn't experience incestuous or sexual relations at home. Theresa hadn't been molested or physically abused at home and her parents weren't drug addicts.

Child sexual exploitation is the most hidden form of child abuse in the United States. Insidious and undetectable, many law enforcement officers and child welfare agencies do not realize the scope of the problem. A retired woman living in a small Ohio lake community with a large number of tourists noticed a young girl across the street that she hadn't seen before. A few days went by and the woman realized that she never saw a school bus coming for the girl in the mornings. Late one night, the woman got up for a drink of water, looked out the window, and saw a number of cars coming and going from the house where the little girl lived. She telephoned the police to report suspicious activity.

The authorities discovered the young girl was being trafficked out of the home by her father. Because of the neighbor's concern, the girl was rescued.

COERCION AND THREATS

The words *option* and *choice* are the opposite of slavery and human trafficking. If we judge that a person has an option, then it cannot be slavery. But bondage can be unseen. Bondage generally is psychological as well as physical.

Many are quick to accuse a girl of having had other options versus having *chosen* a life of prostitution. Did plantation slaves have other options in the 1700's? While owned by a master, they lived in a small home or shack, and were provided with a set of clothing, a bed, and food. They were beaten if they didn't do as told. For the most part they were not daily kept in shackles. But their bondage, like the bondage of modern slaves, was psychological as well as physical.

Could they have run away? Escaped? Some did. Theoretically, escape was an option. Some survived their escape but a great many did not. Is life in bondage better than life-threatening punishment or death? Escape didn't mean instant freedom. It meant:
- their predators would hunt them
- severe punishment if caught

- they had to leave family
- traveling into an unknown region
- an unknown future
- being alone with no money and no one to trust

Today if a child in a third world nation is kidnapped and forced to work on a plantation, could the child run away? If a young woman is brought from another country to be a maid in an exclusive, rich neighborhood, yet she is beaten and sexually assaulted, doesn't know the language, our laws, or how to use a phone, does she truly have options? If somehow she was able to access a phone, could she call the police? Simply leave when the owners were away from the house? Where would she go? Who could she trust for help?

Whether forced prostitution or labor trafficking, modern day slaves are held in psychological bondage. Fear is a major factor, induced by coercion, force, and threats.

Twenty years ago, society believed a woman who was a victim of domestic violence could simply walk away. Outsiders judged that she chose to stay in the situation and deserved the treatment she received. Through education and awareness, we now understand what occurs for the woman mentally.

She must:
- be ready to leave
- feel she has another option that is better than what she is living through
- be certain her children will be protected
- have assurance she will be safe from her abuser
- have means to provide for her herself and her children

Statistics show that many women that fled domestic violence were stalked and killed by their abuser. Victims are aware that they are in a dangerous setting and cognizant that running away may prove life threatening. Without intervention from strong protectors, for these victims there is no good choice.

Traffickers, pimps, violent husbands and boyfriends, and molesters are extremely skilled in making a person feel loved, abusing the victim for their selfish pleasure, apologizing, and starting the toxic cycle over with a few gestures that make the victim feel loved again. All the while the predator assures the victim that they have no choice but to live in silence and make the best of the situation. The tactics are so insidious that the victim believes him.

Why is it difficult for society to blame the perpetrators rather than the victim? Theresa speaks to groups nationally and internationally to bring awareness to the general public of human trafficking. In all her speaking engagements, no one voiced fury at the men who used and abused this young teen. Surprisingly, plenty blamed Theresa for not choosing to escape. This naïve judgment re-victimizes victims like Theresa. The message to victims is:

- You had choices.
- You willingly chose to stay in the situation.
- You deserved to be abused.
- Your abusers are not to be blamed.

This response is a major reason why many victims remain silent. The public must accept that this heinous crime happens:

- close to home
- to someone they know
- to their loved ones

Refusing to hold traffickers and johns guilty for enslaving, exploiting, and abusing others is a form of denial. Without boundaries and repercussions, bullies hurt more people.

THE SOLUTION

If consumers understood that a particular soccer ball was made with child slave labor and didn't purchase the ball, would trafficking in child labor stop? Are corporations willing to exchange higher profits for products that are made without forced or child labor? Are buyers willing to pay more for soccer balls made by free people paid fairly for their skills? How does a shopper know if a soccer ball or any other product is made by slave labor?

APPS TO FIGHT CHILD LABOR

APPLICATIONS ARE AVAILABLE FOR DOWNLOAD ON PHONES THAT TELL THE STORY BEHIND EACH BARCODE. THESE APPS PROVIDE CONSUMERS WITH INFORMATION ON HOW PRODUCTS RELATE TO MODERN DAY SLAVERY AND WHAT YOUR FAVORITE BRANDS ARE DOING TO ALLEVIATE FORCED AND CHILD LABOR. (VISIT WWW.FREE2WORK.ORG)

Some items you might use, eat, or wear every day that have a high probability of being produced by a child or person forced into labor include:
- Artificial flowers – China
- Bricks, cement, stone – Afghanistan, Bangladesh, India, North Korea, Pakistan, Paraguay, Peru
- Carpets – Afghanistan, India
- Christmas decorations – China
- Clothing, cotton – Argentina, China, Malaysia, Philippines, Thailand, Zambia

- Coffee – Columbia, El Salvador, Nigeria, Peru, Uganda
- Cocoa (chocolate) – Columbia, Peru
- Diamonds, sapphires, emeralds, gems, gold – Angola, Columbia, Madagascar, Peru, Sierra Leone, Zambia
- Electronics – China
- Fireworks – China, El Salvador, Peru
- Footwear – Bangladesh, China
- Nuts – Bolivia
- Rice – India, Uganda
- Rubber (for tires, flip flops, etc.) – Burma, Indonesia
- Shrimp, fish – Bangladesh, Cambodia, El Salvador, Thailand
- Soccer balls – India
- Sugar – Brazil, El Salvador, Pakistan, Thailand, Uganda
- Tea – Rwanda, Uganda
- Toys – China
- Zinc (for computers and cell phones) – Bolivia

Trader Joes, Whole Foods, farmers markets, and stores that produce and sell locally made items feature products that do not involve slave labor. Many organic items are also fair trade. Companies labeled Rain Forest

Certified, Fair Trade, or Organic allow others onto their property to speak to employees, and pay employees a fair market price for their work. Other labels are Fair for Life, Equal Exchange, and Whole Trade. There are also many organizations that train survivors and give them a skill, and the products they make and sell help support them.

SUMMARY

The average age of entry into trafficking in the U.S. is 13. Most trafficked children have been abused at home or come from impoverished or broken families. While it may appear that victims of labor or sex trafficking have an option to escape or tell someone, the truth is that they don't feel they can because of extreme consequences and threats.

FREEDOM FIGHTERS CHALLENGE

GO THROUGH YOUR HOME AND NOTE THE COUNTRIES WHERE YOUR CLOTHES, FOOD, SHOES, TOYS, AND OTHER BELONGINGS CAME FROM. WE CONSUME MANY ITEMS MADE BY PEOPLE THAT WERE NOT PAID FOR THEIR WORK. AS CONSCIOUS CONSUMERS, WE CAN LOWER THE DEMAND FOR CHEAP GOODS AND ENSURE THAT WE DON'T CONTRIBUTE TO MODERN DAY SLAVERY.

CHAPTER SEVEN

FUELED BY GREED

IN THIS CHAPTER:
ECONOMICS 101
NO WAY OUT
BLAMING THE VICTIM

Greed is not a financial issue. Greed is a heart issue.
— Andy Stanley

AS A TEENAGER, Theresa was brought into these men-only dens. When her eyes adjusted to the smoke and darkness, she saw coffee tables piled with drinks, cigarettes, and large stacks of cash. Clearly a business transaction had been arranged prior to her arrival.

Theresa's understanding was that she was working off the price of the photographs and protecting her family from harm. She was a child trying to trade herself for humiliating photos of her attacker's abuse.

The traffickers never negotiated a price for the photos because they never intended to give them to Theresa. Those images were leverage her traffickers employed to control Theresa as long as she proved profitable to them. Blackmail.

ECONOMICS 101

Human trafficking is an economic relationship. It's about money and greed.

Imagine you have a craving for chocolate and only $3 in your pocket. Would you buy a large bag of chocolate although you don't know where the cocoa came from or one Certified Fair Trade chocolate bar? Most people are inclined to grab the large bag and get more for their money. Unfortunately, this fuels the slave market.

When chocolate companies purchase cocoa, they generally look for the largest quantity for the cheapest price – the same way our shopper above chose the large bag over the single bar. Focused on keeping prices low while making more profit, companies may not consider whether the workers who collected and processed the cocoa were kidnapped, forced to work on plantations, beaten, and not paid. The demand for chocolate is especially high around Valentines Day, Easter, Halloween, and Christmas. Demand fuels human trafficking.

Although Theresa did not realize this at the time,

she was used as a reward and incentive for others to perform better or produce more. She was an illegal prize to motivate productivity. This only worked because the johns, as well as the traffickers, operated without any sense of compassion, ethics, or the moral compass that sets humans apart from animals.

TRICKY TRAFFICKERS

HAVE YOU EVER BEEN TRICKED INTO DOING SOMETHING YOU REALLY DIDN'T WANT TO DO? TRAFFICKERS TRICK THEIR VICTIMS BY:

- EARNING THEIR TRUST
- BLACKMAIL
- TURNING VIOLENT

Years after the event, a 40-year-old woman wrote to tell Theresa of her story. One night her boyfriend took her out supposedly on a date. At an isolated rest stop several men bound her, pulled a bag over her head, and assaulted her sexually. The man she assumed cared about her, sold her for the entire weekend to pay off a debt he owed. Humiliated and ashamed, bruised and broken, she didn't tell anyone what had happened. Because she was embarrassed, she kept his criminal act a secret. By keeping his secret, this woman allowed him and her abusers to get away with hurting her and encouraged them to exploit other girls in the future for money.

Because traffickers aim to have complete control over someone's identity, victimization can potentially happen anywhere and to anyone. In reality, Theresa *belonged* to her trafficker although it seemed as if she belonged to the cousin who pretended to be romantically interested in her. In reality, the cousin was the recruiter and groomer.

Traffickers come from all socioeconomic and racial characteristics, though it is more common among cultures that don't value women. Traffickers range from familial operations to highly organized international networks that are connected with contacts in many cities.

As a little girl, Charlotte idolized her older brother. But he began doing drugs and Charlotte hid in her room when strange men came for parties at their house when her mom was away. Eventually her brother sold Charlotte to the men who came to the house to pay for his drug habit. Because he threatened Charlotte not to tell anyone, her mother had no idea what was happening to her daughter while she was at work.

Experts at beating down their victim with emotional and mental abuse until they are too frightened to tell anyone, the tools of traffickers include force, torture, manipulation, and coercion. Psychologically and physically, the message is the same: the victim is valueless. Worthless. Slavery is about controlling people for another's selfish gain.

If the men involved had viewed Theresa as the valuable young girl she was, they would never have considered hurting her. When people choose to honor and respect each other in the same way that they want to be treated, traffickers can set up business but no one – no johns – will show up. No money will be exchanged and no children or adults will be victimized.

NO WAY OUT

In addition to the economic (money) factor, another core characteristic of slavery is violence. As traffickers exert control over a person through violence, victims either have no choice or feel like they have no option but to submit. The victim no longer has free will. Theresa had to do as she was told or she was severely punished. The traffickers threatened to harm or kill her loved ones and for Theresa, that was not an option.

Once in, the victim is usually enslaved until death. The most common means to freedom for most victims are death from the following:

- drug overdose
- vicious beatings
- untreated illness
- suicide (If given the opportunity, a victim may commit suicide rather than endure the continuing nightmare.)

The tragic reality is that escape and rescue are extremely rare for a person who is trafficked. A few age out, which means a victim may be strong enough to survive and traffickers abandon the victim in favor of grooming a new and younger person. Occasionally a victim becomes very ill or is tossed out as traffickers find a more beneficial initiate.

BLAMING THE VICTIM

It is extremely challenging for Americans to comprehend the reality of slavery in the United States. Most would prefer to turn away, deny it happens, or re-victimize the survivor by not believing their experience, requiring them to prove their story, or stating they must have had a choice. Doesn't everyone in America have free will? This is the land of the free, right? Surely everyone has options and choices, right?

Unfortunately, that is not the case.

Theresa boldly shares her story as a girl from the suburbs who was manipulated, coerced, and threatened into terrible things against her will while others profited. Since Theresa began speaking publicly, others have felt safe to confess their own similar, sad stories.

In 2009 on the *Today Show*, Theresa's seven-minute interview aired for the first time on national television. Within minutes, Internet posts swamped the website with comments of disbelief. Some stated there 'were holes in her story,' she was 'crying wolf,' and trying to get revenge on the trafficker. The segment was a teaser for a feature on MSNBC *Sex Slaves: The Teen Trade* at a later date. But the damage was done. Theresa and other survivors read the comments. After years of being trafficked, survivors with advanced college degrees are still labeled as the "ex-stripper" or "ex-prostitute". While it may seem that there are not many victims, most survivors are too ashamed and afraid of what others will think about them if they tell their story.

Human trafficking happens to children and teens in cities and small towns across the United States. The victims are children of every color, every socioeconomic background, with two parents, or no parents. Sexual slavery can happen to anyone.

SUMMARY

Modern day slavery can happen to anyone in the United States. Trafficking victims are kept silent by threats and violence. The bonds of slavery are physical and psychological. Many victims are too ashamed to share their stories and ostracized when they do.

FREEDOM FIGHTERS CHALLENGE

THE SIGNS OF SEXUAL EXPLOITATION ARE NOT EASY TO SEE. THIS ALLOWS HUMAN TRAFFICKING TO OCCUR IN OUR OWN NEIGHBORHOODS. BE WILLING TO CARE. YOU MAY SAVE A LIFE.

CHAPTER EIGHT

WHEN ARE PEOPLE TRAFFICKED?

IN THIS CHAPTER:
LOCATION, LOCATION, LOCATION
THE PROCESS

> *Creation is an ongoing process, and when we create a*
> *perfect world where love and compassion are shared by all,*
> *suffering will cease.*
> — *Bernie Siegel*

ON HER WAY HOME from work one day, a mom noticed that a small item that had been left behind in the window of an abandoned house had been moved. She knew no one had purchased the house so she called the local police. "I noticed a change in the abandoned house in my neighborhood," she said, "and wanted to let you know in case it meant something."

The police stopped by and found traffickers inside.

A young girl was rescued because a woman was observant and willing to care about her neighbors.

LOCATION, LOCATION, LOCATION

• As long as the demand exists, people are at risk. The perpetual rise of trafficking proves that there is no shortage of cruel people that will ensnare and enslave others, no shortfall of evil men intent on exploiting young girls. And their greed is never satisfied.

Several factors make a location susceptible to trafficking, either as a destination place or a transit site:
  • proximity to an international border
  • extensive highway systems
  • truck stops
  • growing immigrant populations
  • proximity to large universities
  • international corporations
  • agricultural industries
  • military bases
  • tourist locations
  • casinos or adult entertainment business

However, these factors do not need to prequalify a location for traffickers. When community members are vigilant, trafficking does not flourish.

THE PROCESS

There are several stages experts have identified as generally employed by traffickers from the point they identify a potential slave to the end of the slavery for that victim.

EXPOSED

Theresa was insecure in her new school and desperate to fit in. Most of all, she craved attention and wanted to be liked. The older student appeared to fulfill those longings through subtle flirting with Theresa.

Traffickers are adept at finding people that can be easily coerced, forced, manipulated, and exploited. People that can be deceived. Traffickers target:

- people without strong support networks
- the disadvantaged
- those in poverty
- the lonely
- children who have been abused
- neglected people
- those that hope and dream of a better future

SCOUTED

Theresa was misled to believe the older boy truly was interested in her as a friend and boyfriend. Once the older student believed Theresa was a good candidate and won her trust, he invited her to get into his car. In the book *Renting Lacey* by Shared Hope, Lacey met a man at the park that she passed each day on her way home from school. He talked to her and gave her compliments. She believed he liked her. After a few months, he asked if he could give her a ride home. But once she got into his car, he didn't take her to her house.

Traffickers mislead victims through the following:

- attention
- gifts
- promises
- false jobs

VACATED

In Theresa's case, the boy garnered her trust until she willingly got into his car. Traffickers lure vulnerable targets by weaving an appealing picture of a future filled with opportunity and security. The trafficker wants the victim to willingly leave behind family and friends and everything familiar and be attached to the trafficker.

TRANSPORTED

Traffickers mercilessly wielded blackmail, threats, and coercion to convince Theresa to leave the safety of her house each night when they telephoned. She was without identification as he drove her away from all she knew to places where she was horribly exploited. To infuse confusion and terror, traffickers transport victims across borders, over state lines, to another city, or a far away neighborhood. In the process, traffickers strip the victim of identity, and ensure submission through physical abuse.

Lacey was taken miles away from her family and had no idea how to return. The man she thought was her boyfriend took her phone and moved her into a house with other girls she didn't know.

REGULATED

Traffickers controlled Theresa through the photos they had taken of her during the rape. One night Theresa didn't answer when the phone rang. The next time she was called into service, she was beaten and told never to ignore their call again or they would kill her brothers. The people who trafficked her controlled Theresa.

Lacey was given different clothes and a new name. She was told when she could eat and sleep and drugged, so the trafficker could control her.

RELOCATED

Each night Theresa was taken to a new place. She did not know where she was, the customs of her captors, or the language the men spoke. She was reliant on the trafficker to return her to her home before morning when Theresa's parents and brothers woke up. Victims are taken to a place where they will be enslaved. They are threatened against communicating their circumstances to anyone.

Many times victims are taken to hotels, dropped off at the front door, and told which room to go to. The trafficker waits outside the hotel and takes the victim to the next motel, with no chance of escape.

OPPRESSED

Theresa's abuse nearly killed her. Victims are forced to work as slaves. Those brought from another country to the United States, with promises of good employment, find themselves forced to work off a debt for their passage that never gets paid. Traffickers impose a perpetual debt on the victim who feels guilty that they allowed themselves to be victimized.

Like Theresa's traffickers who had no intention of ever giving her those photos, traffickers keep victims enslaved because they make money on them.

RESOLVED

Theresa's enslavement came to a fortunate and rare end when her family relocated to another state. Aware that her traffickers might kidnap her, Theresa was careful to keep news of the move to herself. Most slaves live a nightmare and die in slavery. A few like Theresa and Lacey are rescued.

SUMMARY

Trafficking can occur in any location and any zip code. States populated with highways, truck stops, military bases, or with a large number of immigrants tend to have an increased number of human trafficking cases. The stages of slavery include the following:

Exposed

Scouted

Vacated

Transported

Regulated

Relocated

Oppressed

Resolved

FREEDOM FIGHTERS CHALLENGE

IF YOU WERE KIDNAPPED OR WOKE TO FIND YOURSELF IN AN UNFAMILIAR CITY, WHAT STEPS WOULD YOU TAKE TO GET HOME? WHAT IF YOU HAD NO MONEY OR CELL PHONE?

CHAPTER NINE

SLAVERY THEN AND NOW

IN THIS CHAPTER:
BRIEF HISTORY
SLAVERY YESTERDAY AND TODAY
ABOLITIONISTS PAST AND PRESENT

Whenever I hear anyone arguing for slavery,
I feel a strong impulse to see it tried on him personally.
— Abraham Lincoln

MITCHELVILLE ON HILTON HEAD ISLAND was a free black community in the South prior to the Emancipation Proclamation.

The first state to secede from the Union on December 20, 1860, South Carolina ignited the Civil War by firing the first shot over Fort Sumter. In the center of the Charleston Bay, the manmade island quickly surrendered to the South.

The North took possession of Hilton Head Island, the largest of the 170 Sea Islands, as a base for blockades against Savannah and Charleston. When the Union soldiers arrived, Southerners who lived on Hilton Head quickly abandoned the island, leaving behind their slaves. Soon, other slaves fled from captivity on the mainland to Hilton Head. Many offered to fight for the North.

Union Major General Ormsby MacNight Mitchel lacked a policy or precedent for including the untrained arrivals in his army, and he would not send them away or treat them as slaves. In 1862, Mitchel gave the newcomers a section of the island where they established their own community and governed themselves.

The Northerners called the setting the Port Royal Experiment.

The former slaves named their new home Mitchelville in honor of the commander who honored their newfound freedom.

Mitchelville residents built a church, laid out streets, and sectioned one-quarter-acre lots. They elected officials, established laws, collected taxes, provided sanitation, and made education compulsory for children ages of 6 through 15.

General Sherman requested assistance from 'highly favored and philanthropic people in the North.' Members of the American Missionary Association and Secretary of the Treasury Salmon P. Chase's associate, Edward L. Pierce, arrived to help Mitchelville residents devise a plan for their welfare and employment.

In April 1862, a military order freed the blacks on the Sea Islands.

On January 1, 1863, President Abraham Lincoln issued the Emancipation Proclamation, freeing all slaves.

By November 1865, Mitchelville had 1,500 residents.

Today, a section of the island is still referred to as Mitchelville and some people in the area can trace their heritage back to that early free community. Without doubt, those that were legally enslaved experienced much of the same emotional and physical trauma that victims of human trafficking feel today.

BRIEF HISTORY

Slavery is not, and never has been, based on the following:

- race
- color
- religion

At its core, slavery targets society's most vulnerable. Slavery is a global example of bullies and the bullied.

Slavery in the United States boasts a particularly unique contradiction. The founding fathers invested their time, talent, and treasure to bring to fruition the

Great American Experiment founded on the declaration that *all men are created equal*. Yet, for the first century of American history, Americans continued to accept and enforce slavery.

LIFE, LIBERTY, AND THE PURSUIT OF HAPPINESS:

THE DECLARATION OF INDEPENDENCE STATES THE FOLLOWING:

"WE HOLD THESE TRUTHS TO BE SELF-EVIDENT: THAT ALL MEN ARE CREATED EQUAL; THAT THEY ARE ENDOWED BY THEIR CREATOR WITH CERTAIN UNALIENABLE RIGHTS; THAT AMONG THESE ARE LIFE, LIBERTY, AND THE PURSUIT OF HAPPINESS."

Following the Civil War and the elimination of slavery, many public places remained segregated including bathrooms, buses, schools, restaurants, jobs, and even water fountains. Racism, a form of bullying, has become an excuse for both whites and blacks to treat each other with disrespect and violence long after the Emancipation Proclamation.

How is modern human trafficking like slavery in bygone years? How is it different?

Living in the area that is now Iraq, the Sumerian populace was divided into freemen and slaves. Conquered people were enslaved and labored for the victors.

Ancient Egypt enslaved great numbers of foreigners and prisoners to construct the labor-intensive pyramids for privileged Egyptians. Moses led the more than a million Hebrew slaves out of Egypt.

Greece conquered more peoples to serve in their households and to fuel their lucrative slave trade.

The Roman Empire consisted of the same number of slaves as freemen. The Romans sold nearly 100,000 Jewish people into slavery. For sport, the Romans trained slaves for combat against brutal animals and each other. Thousands of spectators filled the Coliseum to watch gladiators fight to the death.

In Africa, tribes enslaved other tribes. In 1441, the European slave trade began when Africans sold other Africans of opposing tribes to Europeans. A Portuguese sea captain brought 12 Africans as a gift to Prince Henry in Lisbon. Africans were quickly prized for their size, strength, and the close proximity of the African continent to obtain more slaves.

When Christopher Columbus discovered the New World, slavery already existed among Native American peoples.

The transatlantic slave trade began in the New World when the first slave ship arrived in the colony of Jamestown and the Europeans accepted African slaves. Colonists quickly preferred African slaves above native peoples. Strong workers, the Africans were easier to control because they did not know the language or the country.

Initially slavery in the United States was based on the economics that slave labor was cheaper than paid laborers.

From the nation's birth, slavery was a volatile source of conflict in the United States. A segment of the population benefitted from slavery while others radically opposed the enslavement of any human beings. Tensions mounted and the United States divided over the issue of slavery.

In England, after a 26-year parliamentary campaign against the slave trade, English politician William Wilberforce saw the passage of the Slave Trade Act of 1807 that abolished the slave trade in the British Empire.

The explosive issue of slavery continued to divide the century-old United States of America. In a bloody Civil War in 1860, whites in the North gave their lives to fight whites in the South to preserve the union of a United States without slavery.

Slavery was outlawed in the United States in 1865 when abolitionist and president Abraham Lincoln issued the Emancipation Proclamation. The freed slaves hailed Lincoln as their Moses.

SLAVERY YESTERDAY AND TODAY

How does slavery in the United States today compare with slavery during the time the founding fathers were establishing the Great American Experiment – the new United States of America?

Race was a contributing factor during the antebellum slave era in the United States. Though the racial issue looks very different in modern slavery, ethnicity played a significant role in who was trafficked. In former eras:

- Slavery in the United States targeted African adults.
- Africans were transported from their own country to the United States.
- Men were valued for their strength and ability to do hard labor.
- Women were used chiefly for domestic work.
- Slaves were easily distinguished from freemen because they looked different.
- Once in the United States, slaves were unfamiliar with the culture and language. They were reliant on their captors.
- Slaves were legally owned.
- Owners kept and maintained a slave and the slave's offspring for long periods, even for a lifetime.
- Slaves were considered an investment, bought for an amount equivalent today of $40,000 to $100,000.

Ways that modern day slavery is different in the U.S.:

- Girls are the primary targets.
- Children are preferred.
- Any race is desirable.
- There is no legal ownership of a slave because slavery in any form is illegal.
- Slaves are used primarily for sex.
- Unfamiliar with our culture, social norms, and language, girls brought from other countries are reliant on their captors.
- Slaves are considered disposable because there are always vulnerable people.
- Slaves are not maintained or expected to survive longer than seven years.
- The internet is used to purchase and sell slaves.
- Girls can be purchased for around $90.00.
- Slaves are moved around the country so they can't be found and can't escape.

 INDIGENOUS *adj.* in·dig·e·nous \in-ˈdi-jə-nəs\ 1. DERIVED FROM THE LATIN "ETYMOLOGY" INDICATING A PERSON THAT IS NATIVE OR BORN WITHIN A PARTICULAR REGION OR LOCATION. SIMILAR WORDS INCLUDE ABORIGINAL, FIRST, NATIVE, AND ORIGINAL.

There are more slaves in the United States now than there were at the peak of the transatlantic slave trade. But modern slaves aren't sold for their ability to do physical labor; they are being forced to have sex with as many as 50 men each day to enrich thug-like sex traffickers.

ABOLITIONISTS PAST AND PRESENT

In the past abolitionists reasoned with the public to reject slavery by publishing convincing arguments that were widely read. Lawmakers lobbied for anti-slavery legislation, and grassroots movements freed as many slaves as they could through the Underground Railroad.

Today:

• Abolitionists raise awareness within their communities, the nation, and around the world.

• Neighborhoods create accountability groups that network with local authorities to protect residents.

• Traffickers prey upon those that are the most vulnerable, and in response churches, faith-based groups, schools, and community organizations strive to empower others, making them less vulnerable.

• Personnel with military training and law enforcement experience volunteer their services to rescue victims.

• Grassroots movements are establishing safe places staffed with trained professionals where victims of trafficking can receive emotional, physical, and mental healing.

• Law enforcement and emergency personnel are trained to recognize signs of trafficking and to intervene.

• New laws target traffickers and johns.

• Theresa Flores courageously shares her story, educating the public, empowering victims, and inspiring people to proactively care for loved ones, communities, the nation, and the world.

SUMMARY

Throughout history, people have been enslaved. Although slavery is currently not legal anywhere, there are more slaves today than at any other time in history. Modern day slavery looks very different from past slavery. Everyone is important in the fight to end human trafficking.

FREEDOM FIGHTERS CHALLENGE

WHAT WILL YOU DO TODAY TOWARD ELIMINATING MODERN SLAVERY?

GROUPS YOU CAN PARTNER WITH INCLUDE

- S.O.A.P. (SAVE OUR ADOLESCENTS FROM PROSTITUTION)
- WOMEN AT RISK INTERNATIONAL (WAR)
- INTERNATIONAL JUSTICE MISSION (IJM)
- POLARIS PROJECT
- DESTINY RESCUE
- TRICKED (FILM PROJECT)
- CALL & RESPONSE
- CHILDREN AND FAMILIES ACROSS BORDERS (CFAB)
- NOT FOR SALE

CHAPTER TEN

THE SOLUTION

IN THIS CHAPTER:
RED FLAG ALERT
MY BROTHER AND SISTER'S KEEPER
LIBERATOR'S AWARD

> *Throughout history, it has been the inaction of those who*
> *could have acted;*
> *the indifference of those who should have known better;*
> *the silence of the voice of justice when it mattered most;*
> *that has made it possible for evil to triumph.*
> — *Halle Selassie*

ON A WINTRY SATURDAY AFTERNOON, a couple's car had a flat tire in front of a motel just outside of a large city. As the man repaired the tire, the woman noticed a car stop at the motel. An African-American teenager about 15 years old got out wearing too much makeup, revealing clothes, and no winter jacket. The girl appeared frightened. A white man in his 50's or 60's got out of the car, took the girl by the arm, unlocked the motel room door, and pushed her inside.

The bystander quickly told her husband what she had seen and they called 9-1-1. Because of that woman's keen observation and compassion when the situation did not look healthy, that 15-year-old was rescued.

RED FLAG ALERT

We are the solution. We share neighborhoods, cities, nations, and the globe. Each of us has a say in what happens in our world. We can make a difference starting with protecting ourselves, caring for our family, and supporting those in our circle of influence. If we choose to turn the other way, then we are choosing for human trafficking to flourish. If allowed to grow, modern slavery will impact everyone.

There is a balance between being nosey, an alarmist, a vigilante, and being responsible. Headlines in California and Ohio reported nearly unbelievable stories about girls that had been kidnapped and kept prisoner for years in neighborhood homes without neighbors noticing. Living in community requires respecting the privacy of others, and being concerned when something does not seem appropriate.

Parents, teachers, principals, coaches, law enforcement officers, medical, and counseling professionals must listen for the child's silent cry. Siblings, peers, friends, neighbors, and fellow community members must trust their intuition when something seems amiss in the life of another. Communities benefit when professionals and neighbors can and will protect children in the neighborhood.

Ignoring the problem and being too cowardly to get involved only validates to the victim that they are worthless, guilty, not valued, and the one at fault. Bullies expand their control to encompass those who chose to ignore their breach of boundaries and accountability.

Be alert to red flags that indicate someone may be bullied. Clues that a person might be a victim of human trafficking include the following:

- indications that they are being controlled by an older person
- bruises, broken bones, concussions, or other signs of physical abuse
- abrasions around the wrists, ankles, or neck
- inability to go to another place without someone's permission
- fear
- depression
- sudden change in behavior

- sudden drop in grades
- new set of friends, particularly older ones who are unfriendly and distant to adults
- new cell phone, expensive jewelry, or other items you know their family could not afford
- frequent, unexplained absences from school
- dropping out of activities they used to enjoy
- out in public without identification or money not knowing where they are
- chronically runs away from home
- makes reference to travel to other cities, but doesn't know specifics about the location
- hungry or malnourished
- inappropriately dressed based on the weather conditions or surroundings. If the weather is hot yet a girl is wearing long sleeves, she may be hiding marks on her body. If temperatures are cold but she is scantily dressed, she may be being victimized.
- signs of drug addiction
- makes reference to sexual situations that are beyond age-specific norm (a challenge these days due to our highly sexual culture)
- has a boyfriend who is noticeably older
- makes reference to terminology of the commercial sex industry

- has hotel keys or large amounts of cash
- numerous pregnancies
- needs treatment for sexually transmitted diseases (STDS)

Environmental signs include:
- locks on the outside of a door (versus inside)
- bars on windows
- people sleeping and working in the same location, and in cramped, over crowded conditions
- sparse living conditions, generally only a mattress on the floor

MY BROTHER AND SISTER'S KEEPER

The adults in Theresa's life chose to do nothing. By turning a blind eye, they allowed themselves to be controlled by this gang and permitted a child in their care to be hurt in ways they could never have imagined.

If you suspect someone needs help, intervention, or rescue, **do** the following:
- Ask the child or person if he or she needs help.
- Talk about your concerns with someone with authority in the situation such as a school counselor, teacher, pastor, youth leader, or the child's parent.
- Call the local authorities and tell them when you see something that looks like it may be trafficking.

If someone appears to be in danger, call 9-1-1.

• Program your state trooper hotline number in your cell phone in case you see anything suspicious while on the road.

• Call the Human Trafficking Hotline when you notice conditions listed above that appear suspicious, 1-888-373-7888.

 NATIONAL HUMAN TRAFFICKING HOTLINE
1-888-373-7888

If you suspect someone needs help, intervention, or rescue, **don't** do the following:

• Assume the worst. When possible, knock on a neighbor's door and ask how they are doing. One family was dismayed to have authorities arrive at their door with a report from neighbors of possible child neglect. The reality was their newborn was hospitalized with a life-threatening condition. With the family focused on the critical condition of the newborn, the yard and other children suddenly looked unkempt compared to the family's normal. Help from the neighbors with yard work and meals would have been more compassionate than suspicion and judgment.

- Report a homeschooling family because their children spend their schooldays at home.
- Assume you are wrong or that someone else will report it. We have an innate sense of danger. Our gut feeling is rarely wrong. If you are wrong about the situation, so what? If you are right, you may be a victim's only chance of freedom.

TIPS FOR PARENTS:

- INSTALL A CELL PHONE LOCATOR ON YOUR CHILD'S CELL PHONE. IF YOUR CHILD IS MISSING, THIS MAY BE THE ONLY TOOL YOU HAVE TO LOCATE THEM.
- INSTALL A HOME SECURITY SYSTEM. MANY ARE AFFORDABLE AND PROVIDE AN ALERT WHENEVER A WINDOW OR DOOR OPENS.
- CHECK YOUR CHILD'S BED EACH NIGHT. DON'T PRESUME YOUR CHILD IS ASLEEP.
- GET THE PHONE NUMBERS OF YOUR CHILD'S FRIENDS' PARENTS. DON'T ASSUME YOU CAN REACH YOUR CHILD AT ANY TIME. WHAT IF A TRAFFICKER TAKES AWAY THE PHONE?

S.O.A.P.

Abolitionists use many methods to free those who are enslaved. Theresa's trademarked program S.O.A.P. (Save Our Adolescents from Prostitution) educates motel and hotel workers on the signs of human trafficking and rescues missing children and victims of labor and sex trafficking.

Funds donated to S.O.A.P. purchase small bars of soap like those used in hotel rooms. Volunteers attach stickers to the label that reads,

Are you being forced to do anything you do not want to do?
Are you being threatened if you try to leave?
Are you witnessing young girls being prostituted?
If so, call 1-888-373-7888.

From her own experience, Theresa knows that the only time trafficked girls are alone may be for a few moments in the bathroom.

Volunteers deliver the complimentary soap and show hotel staff photos of missing children provided through agencies such as Crimes Against Children, Child Rescue Network and the National Center for Missing and Exploited Children.

Occasionally a hotel clerk recognizes someone from the photos. "I see her in here all the time." The staff did not realize that the girl was being trafficked but now she can be rescued.

During the S.O.A.P. outreach to hotels prior to the Super Bowl in Phoenix, Arizona, a front desk clerk recognized one of the missing teens from the poster. The 15-year-old had checked into the hotel the night before with her "boyfriend". S.O.A.P. coordinators notified police, and within 24 hours two teens were rescued. The boyfriend was actually a wanted trafficker authorities had been pursuing and was taken into custody.

Abolitionists know that human trafficking dramatically increases in an area during a large event that draws crowds of people. Volunteers canvas hotels and deliver soap in the weeks prior to the Super Bowl, New Year's Eve events, golf and Nascar events, and even the World's Strongest Man competition.

"Has anyone been rescued as a result of the S.O.A.P. project?" someone asked at a workshop for victims.

"I don't know," Theresa admitted.

"I know." A girl at the table raised her hand. "Six months ago, I was in danger and locked myself in the hotel bathroom and called that number. The police came and rescued me."

While there is no way to know how many victims

have found and used the phone number on the small bar of soap, several people have reported that they did call for help and were rescued as a result of the S.O.A.P. Project.

Including grassroots organizations, non-governmental organizations (NGO), churches, ad hoc groups, and lawmakers, people across the nation and around the world are working to eradicate the crime of human trafficking. Ex-special forces use their training to partner with groups that rescue victims, individuals watchdog their neighborhoods, and facilities are established to help victims recover and reenter life as a free person.

Modern day abolitionists:
- bring awareness to society about trafficking
- re-educate the public about modern slavery
- reframe beliefs regarding prostitution

Abolitionists commit time, talent, and treasure to eradicate human trafficking by:
- giving a voice to the voiceless
- changing the public mentality
- sounding the alarm that there is limited time to save those who can't save themselves

Some national and international groups dedicated to the eradication of human trafficking include:

- A21
- All Worthy of Love
- Be Free
- Call & Response
- Destiny Rescue
- ECPAT
- Forgotten Children International
- Free the Slaves
- Global Centurion
- International Justice Mission
- LCCAHT (Low Country Coalition Against Human Trafficking)
- Love 146
- Not for Sale
- Polaris Project
- Rescue and Restore
- Second Chance Toledo
- Shared Hope International
- S.O.A.P. (Save Our Adolescents from Prostitution)
- Soroptimist International
- Traffick911
- Truckers Against Trafficking
- Women at Risk International (WAR)

To acknowledge those who create a significant difference in the world by championing freedom from slavery, Theresa and fellow abolitionists founded the Liberator Awards. This yearly recognition goes to a person who did outstanding work to free society of human trafficking. Nominations are made each October by peers, and finalists are determined by popular vote. Winners are revealed at the awards ceremony each January in the categories of:

- Student or Student Organization
- Volunteer
- Individual
- Organization/Church or Civic Group
- Elected Official or Law Enforcement
- Survivor
- Hero-Liberator of the Year

Learn more at www.liberatorawards.com.

SUMMARY

Temper awareness and concern with respect for the freedom and privacy of others. Learn the red flags of human trafficking and make a plan of what you are comfortable doing in case you see the signs. There are organizations in each state like the ones listed in this chapter that bring awareness and fight human trafficking. Organizations are a group of people that combine efforts to make a difference in the world.

FREEDOM FIGHTERS CHALLENGE

WHAT EVENTS ARE SCHEDULED TO BRING IN LARGE NUMBERS OF PEOPLE TO YOUR AREA? CONTACT S.O.A.P. AT WWW.TRAFFICKFREE.COM AND ARRANGE TO BLANKET YOUR COMMUNITY WITH THE NATIONAL HUMAN TRAFFICKING HOTLINE NUMBER. EDUCATE YOUR COMMUNITY AND ERADICATE HUMAN TRAFFICKING.

CHAPTER ELEVEN

SOCIAL CONTRIBUTORS

IN THIS CHAPTER:
ADVERTISING
TRAFFICKERS: TRICK OR TREAT?
ENTERTAINMENT

What one generation tolerates, the next generation will embrace.
— John Wesley

HAVE YOU THOUGHT about how you may be contributing to the enslavement of another human being? Could you be a factor in the exploitation of a child?

Society contributes to the trafficking of children. From children's toys to Halloween costumes to blatant and disturbing media commercials and advertisements, human trafficking is mainstreamed into culture. People are accepting this as regular fare into our communities.

ADVERTISING

Advertising has rapidly become exploitive of girls. A quick glance at marketing campaigns reveals an unvaried menu of images of girls in suggestive poses and clothing. The female form is used to sell everything from cars to vitamin water.

Billboards are rampant along highways and feature larger-than-life-size pictures of males and females in various stages of undress. These advertisements give the appearance that:

- girls are available at any time for sex
- you will look like this or get to be with a person like this if you only buy that product

Men are included in these revealing advertisements, but the majority feature females. Girls are not represented with privacy and honor, but media implies that others are entitled to view and have access to her body at all times.

Advertisements for popular lingerie stores are nothing more than pornography photos. Underage girls appear in sexy underwear, adult hair and makeup, and pouty expressions that have a sexual connotation. Models for these companies report that there is a lot of sexual exploitation in their industry.

Concurrently, clothing manufacturers produce attire

that is ever more formfitting, skimpy, and see-through. Bathing suits cover less than underclothes and society has come to accept that complete strangers are entitled to view a girl's nearly naked form.

It is possible for girls to dress modestly, comfortably, and attractively simultaneously. Mysteriously leaving something for the imagination is healthy in male and female relationships and encourages respect between the sexes.

Consumers influence designers by what they purchase. As in human trafficking, money is a controlling factor. Choose to purchase clothing that does not exploit, and send a strong message to retailers that there is a demand for items that flatter and honor girls. Buyers provide the demand and stores will provide the supply.

CONSUMER CHOICES:

WINTER SCARVES, HATS, MITTENS AND COATS ARE NOT IN DEMAND IN WARM-WEATHER FLORIDA. HOWEVER, SWIMSUITS, SHORTS, FLIP-FLOPS, AND SUNGLASSES ARE TOP SELLERS. WHAT WOULD HAPPEN IF SKIMPY CLOTHING NEVER LEFT THE RACK AT CLOTHING STORES? IF CONSUMERS REFUSED TO PURCHASE REVEALING OUTFITS? WOULD THE DEMAND BE HIGH OR LOW? HOW WOULD STORES MOST LIKELY RESPOND?

TRAFFICKERS: TRICK OR TREAT?

Costumes for pimps, sexy ladies, and streetwalkers are overly popular during Halloween. Glamorizing the pimp culture and victims paints human trafficking with acceptability. There are even 'junior mac daddy' pimp costumes for youth.

In reality, a pimp is a criminal. Pimps are felons, rapists, kidnappers, and molesters. Halloween costumes of streetwalkers depict an inaccurate view and harm victims. The myth is that these women have designer clothing, great shoes, go to fun parties, travel the world, and enjoy this lifestyle. The reality is that she is sold to 20 men each night. She doesn't keep the money she makes because the pimp takes it. She is beaten, drugged, and raped repeatedly until she loses consciousness. She has no freedom, choices, or options. Her life and body are not her own because she is a sex slave.

The sales of video games that glamorize the exploitation and murder of girls have been on the rise. Since its debut in 1997, the video game *Grand Theft Auto* has sold nearly 150 million units. In the game, the player takes on the role of a criminal who roams freely around a big city carrying out various missions such as bank robberies and assassinations. To garner life points, players have sex with prostitutes and receive more points if the player kills her. In version 5, players go to a strip club and get a lap dance.

Other games such as *Pimp War and Saints Row* are equally damaging. Players live the mentality of those who traffick human beings. These games are rated M for Mature, yet are played predominantly by youth. The behavior acted out in these video games is not good for men or youth to practice, nor is it respectful of females.

DANGEROUS MESSAGES?

WHAT MESSAGE DO GAMES LIKE THIS SAY TO YOUNG BOYS? CAN A GAME WITHOUT THE USE OF VIOLENCE AND SEX STILL BE FUN TO PLAY?

ENTERTAINMENT

When did you last watch a movie or television show where the dating couple waits to have sex until they are married? Do men protect the innocence, purity, and reputation of the females in their lives or feel entitled to sex even when the girl is not his wife?

The entertainment industry changes culture. Movies introduce clothing styles and life choices that six months later have become the norm. Female actresses in adventure films become less dressed as the story progresses. Similarly, in film, dating is synonymous with having sex. Yet marriage was designed to provide security and exclusivity to the relationship as a strong and respectful foundation for living life together and raising a family.

Humans are designed to bond sexually, to imprint with another through an exclusive physical union. When that process is interrupted through sex outside a commitment of marriage, honor and respect for the partner is lost. Each relationship break weakens a person's ability to connect and bond to a mate. This cycle leads to generations with attachment disorder – people that have difficulty forming close relationships.

SUPPLY AND DEMAND:

IN THE 1980'S, THE FILM INDUSTRY PRODUCED A LARGE NUMBER OF R-RATED MOVIES AND MOST FAMILIES WITH YOUNG CHILDREN SPENT LESS TIME IN THE THEATER. IN 2001, DISNEY PRODUCED THE G-RATED FEATURE FILM TITLED *PRINCESS DIARIES* AND AUDIENCES FLOCKED TO THE THEATERS. THROUGH THEIR TICKET PURCHASES, THE PUBLIC SENT THE INDUSTRY A POWERFUL VOTE IN FAVOR OF FAMILY-FRIENDLY ENTERTAINMENT, IGNITING A STREAM OF FILMS THAT APPEALED TO A VARIETY OF AGES. THROUGH THE SAME LAW OF SUPPLY AND DEMAND THAT PROPELS THE HUMAN TRAFFICKING INDUSTRY, CONSUMERS DIRECT SUPPLIERS BASED ON WHERE WE GIVE OUR ATTENTION AND OUR MONEY.

SUMMARY

The glamorization of sex and pimps influences everyday life from the clothes we buy to the television shows we watch, from the magazines at the grocery store checkout to toys and video games. Perversion is portrayed as normal in our life and we can't get away from it. The result is that we have become numb to things that used to be unacceptable. We accept sex, pimps, and violence as normal in advertising and entertainment.

FREEDOM FIGHTERS CHALLENGE

CONSIDER CONTEMPORARY ...

- TOYS
- MAGAZINES
- VIDEO GAMES
- TV SHOWS
- FEATURE FILMS
- MUSIC
- INTERNET

WHICH ONES ARE ENCOURAGING AND INSPIRING? WHAT ONES DEADEN YOUR NATURAL MODESTY AND MORALITY?

IF THIS TREND CONTINUES, WHAT WILL THESE LISTED ITEMS LOOK LIKE FOR YOUR CHILDREN? WHAT BEHAVIORS ARE UNACCEPTABLE NOW THAT MAY BE EMBRACED LATER?

CHAPTER TWELVE

LAWS AND LEGALITIES

IN THIS CHAPTER:
LAWS THAT DON'T EXIST
LAWS THAT ENDANGER VICTIMS
NOT BLACK AND WHITE

> *We hold these truths to be self-evident, that all men are created equal, that they are endowed by their Creator with certain unalienable Rights, that among these are Life, Liberty and the pursuit of Happiness.*
> — *The Declaration of Independence*

OHIO IS FIFTH IN THE NATION in trafficking because we have such an intricate interstate system. Toledo is a hub of trafficking. You might not think of a Midwest city that way, but human trafficking happens there. The more aware people are of modern slavery, the more opportunity we have to save our young girls.

Surprisingly, there are issues related to human trafficking that are not clearly right and wrong but are continuing fodder for discussion.

ENTERTAINMENT

Human trafficking is a direct and blatant violation of our natural feelings regarding what is fair and just. Inherently, we know that owning another person as property forced to do a master's bidding is unethical. It is immoral for people to bully another. No one desires to be bullied and human trafficking is the quintessential bullying.

Can lawmakers legislate morality?

In truth, all laws legislate morality because each dictates the moral and ethical behavior of people as they dwell together in community. What people do and don't do equals moral behavior. Laws specify that it is wrong to steal, damage property that belongs to someone else, and to kill. The Declaration of Independence written by our forefathers declares that the United States government was established to protect the right of each individual to life, liberty, and the pursuit of happiness.

Should people be allowed to sell:

- their own kidney?
- someone else's kidney?
- themselves?
- their child?

It is legal for a person to volunteer to donate his own kidney to someone who needs the organ to survive. Some argue that to make it legal to donate a kidney but illegal to sell a kidney is akin to a firefighter going into a burning building to save lives only when the firefighter volunteers the service but not when the firefighter is paid to save lives.

In the Philippines, most men in some villages have a scar on their side. Rather than continue to live in poverty, they have chosen to sell a kidney for more money than they might hope to see in a lifetime. Some invest their funds into a business venture that will support the family for years to come. Many spend the money on temporary pleasures and, before long, return to the same lifestyle prior to selling an organ.

Because it is not legal to sell kidneys, those who arrange for transplant material coach donors to say the kidney is going to a friend or family member. That friend or family member, in turn, is not purchasing the organ, but giving a monetary gift as a token of appreciation. Due to the questionable arrangements, all the promised funds may arrive or only a percentage. The degree of testing and education for the donor is not always as encompassing as it could be, and occasionally someone gives up a vital kidney before knowing he has kidney disease. Now, his one diseased kidney is not adequate to support life long term, and the recipient of his kidney has exchanged one failing kidney for another.

- Should a man living in poverty be able to give a kidney in exchange for enough money to bring his family out of poverty so they can buy property as well as pigs and chickens for an ongoing means of support?
- Are people who are more knowledgeable and have superior resources taking advantage of the poverty of others?
- Are kidney brokers offering hope to both a sick person and a poor person?
- Is the broker of kidneys trafficking human organs?

SOMETHING TO THINK ABOUT:

WHY CAN WE SELL OUR EGGS BUT NOT OUR KIDNEYS?

Currently women can sell their reproductive eggs. These eggs are used in research and to create babies for those with reproductive challenges. Students at prestigious colleges receive a higher price for their eggs. If it is legal to sell her eggs, should a woman be able to sell her baby? Her body? Her kidney?

Human trafficking is the selling of one human being for the benefit of another. People naturally feel this is wrong because each person has value and potential. Trafficking steals the ability of a human being to live life. No one desires to be trafficked.

LAWS THAT ENDANGER VICTIMS

In an effort to curtail prostitution, states outlawed brothels – businesses where girls were trafficked. Instead of ending the sex trafficking of young women, traffickers coerced girls to stand on the streets and solicit johns who continued to purchase sex. The dilemma these laws created was that girls experienced a vestige of protection when johns came to brothels. But girls picked up on streets by strangers had no such protection from additional violence. Do laws that forbid brothels help trafficking victims?

During World War II, prisoners of war were imprisoned at a military base in the small northern California town of Benicia. Each Friday night, the prisoners were marched from the arsenal to a brothel on Main Street. Did this common practice encourage immorality or protect American girls from being exploited?

In an effort to curtail trafficking and prostitution, authorities remove Internet sites where girls post their availability and network with one another. There is a flip side of shutting down these communication centers.

"We could report to each other if a john was unkind or dangerous," one girl said. "Taking down sites silences sex workers. Being silenced keeps sex workers from the protection of police."

Will trafficking go the way of abortion and drugs that once were illegal but now are sanctioned?

NOT BLACK AND WHITE

Traffickers report that white, Hispanic, and Asian girls are easier to control than their black counterparts. However, traffickers who are arrested with black victims report more often being charged with pimping and pandering while traffickers who are arrested with white girls are more often charged with trafficking.

Originating with the early enslavement of people from Africa, there has long been a tension in the United States between African Americans and Caucasians. Division between people groups is not unique to America. Every nation has prejudice about people of another ethnicity.

- Is trafficking less of a crime depending on the race of the victim?
- Are some humans less valuable than others?

Demand has become so encompassing for labor and sex trafficking that anyone is vulnerable. Girls of all colors, body sizes, and hair color are sold equally on-line. Boys, girls, and people from all nations are suscep-tible to kidnapping and forced to work without wages.

SUMMARY

Although U.S. law forbidding human trafficking was enacted in 2000, many states still arrest the victim but permit pimps, johns, or traffickers to go free. People have the ability to do what they want with their own body within certain legal limits, but laws are designed to protect the vulnerable from bullies, even though that isn't always the case.

FREEDOM FIGHTERS CHALLENGE

WHAT LAWS ALREADY EXIST IN YOUR STATE THAT PROTECT INDIVIDUALS FROM ENSLAVEMENT? SHOULD SOCIETY IMPLEMENT ADDITIONAL LAWS TO STOP THE TRAVESTY OF HUMAN TRAFFICKING THAT DESTROYS LIVES AND FAMILIES?

CHAPTER THIRTEEN

VICTIM-PROOF YOUR LIFE

IN THIS CHAPTER:
STAY SAFE
ACCOUNTABILITY
EXERCISE CAUTION

*Is life so dear or peace so sweet as to be purchased at the price
of chains and slavery? ... but as for me, give me liberty,
or give me death!*
— *Patrick Henry*

IT WAS A RECURRING NIGHTMARE. What choice would
Theresa make if she could save a life by sacrificing her
own? In the dream she was confronted in a dark alley,
a convenience store, or parking garage. Would she jump
in front of a bullet for a stranger? If needed, could she
freely give her life for another?

Theresa's dream became reality when every day for

two years she had to make the decision. Would she tarnish her family's name? Allow her siblings and parents to be harmed? As a child faced with life threatening decisions, she chose her family. Believing she was protecting those she loved, Theresa endured sexual slavery. Despite the horror, she never wavered in her decision.

STAY SAFE

Theresa's fate does not have to be yours. Here are proactive behaviors that young people can do to stay safe.

- Treat people, and yourself, with dignity.
- Stay away from questionable settings.
- Always ask "What if?" What if my drink gets drugged? What if the ride home he is offering doesn't take me home?
- Be watchful and aware of the people around you. Put distance between you and anyone that makes you feel like something is odd – not quite right.
- Never participate in sexting. Never send revealing, suggestive, or inappropriate photos or messages of yourself.
- Block and do not receive inappropriate photos from others.
- Avoid pornography. Be aware of what you

allow your eyes to see and your mind to focus on. Remember that porn changes your brain, ruins your relationships, is addictive, and will control you. Pornography is the root of sex trafficking.

• Create a group of friends and agree together to stay in school, be productive with your lives, and remain untangled from drugs, alcohol, and pornography. Live life full and free.

• Add a computer nanny to your computer to protect from accidentally encountering porn sites.

• Block and clear apps from your phone that are porn related.

• Have a 'no tolerance' stance on porn, bullying, and human trafficking.

• Use your computer in common rooms of your home where family members are aware of what you are viewing.

• Give your computer and phone passwords to your parents. Agree that your parent can periodically check your history.

• Have conversations with your parent about who you communicate with.

• Say no to anything that makes you feel uncomfortable.

- Say no to anything you don't want to do.
- Make certain a parent or other trusted adult always knows where you are.
- Always carry identification.
- Install GPS tracking on your cell phone.
- Limit overnighters. You sleep better at home in your own bed.

ACCOUNTABILITY

Partner with your parents and the trustworthy adults in your life to keep you safe from sexual predators, molesters, and those who traffic human beings. Stay connected and help your parents know:

- your world and your interests
- who you spend time with
- where you are
- where you are going
- the address and phone number where you will be
- that you are asleep in your bed at night
- that parents are there if you spend the night with friends
- where to drop you off
- when to pick you up

Be thankful that your parents care when they are involved in school activities and extracurricular events.

EXERCISE CAUTION

Here are red flags that warn you are placing yourself in potential danger:

- Conversations you don't want your parent to know about
- Relationship(s) you keep secret
- Going places you know are off-limits
- Giving in when someone says, "It's okay, your mom/dad won't know."
- If anyone tells you not to tell your parent about something
- Going against family rules and standards
- Accepting gifts you won't tell your parent about
- Involvement with drugs and alcohol
- Anything requiring you to lie, hide, or keep secret

SUMMARY

Anyone that purposefully deceives and harms another is a bully and is responsible for their actions.

While it may not be possible to completely bully-proof your life, you can be proactive with wise lifestyle choices.

FREEDOM FIGHTERS CHALLENGE

LIVE WISELY AND YOUR EXAMPLE WILL ENCOURAGE OTHERS TO MAKE GOOD CHOICES.

CHAPTER FOURTEEN

RESCUED

IN THIS CHAPTER:
RELEASE
RESIDUAL REMINDERS
RECOVERY

There's a special evil in the abuse and exploitation
of the most innocent and vulnerable.
— President George W. Bush

THERESA SLOUCHED DOWN IN THE SEAT. On moving day, her father drove their blue and white van away from the house in Birmingham. Holding her breath, she prayed no one saw her leave.

As the distance between her family and her traffickers widened, Theresa finally allowed herself to close her eyes and she slept deeply for the first time in years. When she woke and saw the sign for the state of

Connecticut, she sighed with relief. They couldn't find her. At last, she was safe.

In a small, gated community, Theresa's family rented a beach house. That summer, Theresa woke early each morning and walked past four houses, past author Stephen King's summer home, to the beach that faced the Atlantic waters of the Long Island Sound.

Atop a large rock that overlooked the ocean, Theresa closed her eyes, felt the sun on her skin, and listened. Mostly she thanked God for her freedom and a second chance at life. And she was sad for the girl who was taking her place back in Detroit.

Despite the months to rest, recovery didn't come easily. Theresa recognized very early that to go on day in and day out, she had to emotionally detach, disassociate, and compartmentalize her life. If she couldn't function, then her captors won again. The emotional scars and nightmares followed her to college and Theresa realized the horrific trauma she experienced had inflicted life-altering wounds.

Though she was overwhelmingly relieved to have escaped, Theresa was dismayed to realize that being trafficked had affected her emotional, physical, and sexual health. Can a victim recover from extreme abuse?

RELEASED

For victims of human trafficking, the chances of survival are slim. The numbers who escape are slimmer. Rescued victims are in desperate need of the following immediately:

- safety
- medical care
- emotional support
- clothes
- skilled counseling
- job skills
- shelter
- dental work
- rest
- nutrition
- documentation

But the struggle doesn't end there. Recovery, healing, and becoming a productive member of society is another challenge. Some can be reunited with their families and others cannot. Where do victims go to heal? What does that process look like?

All victims, regardless of their age when the victimization began, how long it endured, or how violent it was, suffer posttraumatic stress disorder (PTSD) and depression. Some are even are diagnosed with borderline personality disorder, attachment disorder, or bipolar. Once free, their bodies can heal, but their minds are broken. Their spirit is lost or wounded.

Victims are broken emotionally and physically. Over half of rescued victims must be treated for sexually transmitted diseases given to them by their abusers. Many are addicted to drugs, have untreated broken bones, suffer from migraines, pregnancies, and forced abortions. Many victims now have children of their own, but their children have been removed by child protective services. This loss can be devastating for the mother.

People that have been trafficked may suffer physically from:

- violence
- rape
- beatings
- malnutrition
- exhaustion
- shock
- drugs

Emotionally, victims can suffer from:

- emotional manipulation
- denial of affection
- loss of dignity and self worth
- stolen identity

Mentally, their suffering can include:

- loss of hope
- suspension of faith
- death of dreams
- disbelief in good overcoming evil
- loss of voice
- disappearance of personal worth and value

Theresa discovered firsthand that such severe trauma leaves an impact. Victims can feel heightened:

- fear
- guilt
- distrust of self and others
- hatred
- hopelessness
- addictions
- loss of self
- shame
- anger
- resentment
- isolation
- depression
- numbed feelings

RECOVERY

Recovery requires therapy with a trained, loving, accepting, knowledgeable therapist. To be effective, counselors must become educated on trafficking, trauma, prostitution, and deprogramming for those that suffer from Stockholm syndrome. Cognitive Behavior Therapy helps the patient reframe incorrect thoughts, reconnect with themselves, and once again merge the physical with the emotional to reconnect their body with their soul.

> **STOCKHOLM SYNDROME:**
>
> ABOUT TEN PERCENT OF VICTIMS EXPERIENCE STOCKHOLM SYNDROME, A PSYCHOLOGICAL PHENOMENON THAT OCCURS WHEN VICTIMS EXPRESS EMPATHY AND SYMPATHY FOR THEIR CAPTORS. THE CONDITION WAS IDENTIFIED IN AUGUST 1973 WHEN EMPLOYEES IN A SWEDISH BANK WERE HELD HOSTAGE IN A VAULT. DURING THE STANDOFF WITH POLICE, THE HOSTAGES BECAME EMOTIONALLY ATTACHED TO THEIR CAPTORS, REJECTED ASSISTANCE FROM GOVERNMENT OFFICIALS, AND DEFENDED THE CRIMINALS AFTER THE SIX-DAY TRAUMA. STOCKHOLM SYNDROME OCCURS WHEN VICTIMS MISTAKE LACK OF ABUSE AS KINDNESS FROM CAPTORS. THE POPULAR FAIRY TALE, *BEAUTY AND THE BEAST*, IS AN EXAMPLE OF STOCKHOLM SYNDROME WHEN BELLE IS HELD HOSTAGE BY THE BEAST BUT EVENTUALLY BECOMES SYMPATHETIC AND THEN FALLS IN LOVE WITH HER CAPTOR.

Successful counseling focuses on trust, security, and self love. Victims tend to respond to their experience in three categories:

1) The victim finds it difficult, if not impossible, to trust others and themselves because they feel that vital people have let them down and been hurtful.

2) A victim may be so desperate for someone special in their life that they too freely trust untrustworthy people. This perpetuates the cycle of being a victim who is victimized which reaffirms they are a victim. Being always on guard, waiting for the next blow, is exhausting.

3) A victim is groomed to believe she has no value or freedom to choose her own life so she relies on others to tell her what to do. This is a transfer of dependence from the abuser to others rather than becoming personally responsible.

- Whether unable to trust or trusting without discernment, many victims find it nearly impossible to love themselves. The combination of intense guilt, shame, and being without a voice and without a name prevents them from developing healthy feelings of self. Unable to trust themselves, they let others make decisions for them but are consistently unhappy with the results. Their world is like a small glass box where they remain trapped, watching everyone else enjoy life.
- It can be difficult for victims to say no to anything they don't want to do because they have not had a voice regarding their own lives and bodies. They have not experienced the safety and dignity of safe boundaries.
- Victims are programmed to appease the anger of others at their own expense.

It took years for Theresa to find a word that described what had happened to her. While getting her counseling degree and working as a social worker, Theresa attended a work-related conference where the speaker described a new trend professionals were beginning to learn about called human trafficking.

Prior, Theresa had attempted to talk to rape counselors and various therapists, but no one had heard of the horror she had experienced. From the conference, Theresa finally had a word for what happened to her. She learned human trafficking was a growing concern and she wasn't the only one.

Theresa learned all she could about the topic. She studied the healing and recovery models. She stopped disassociation and burying feelings and memories and faced her past. Theresa began to find herself again. She had not been abused because she was not valuable, but because there were evil men that exploited and hurt children.

Part of Theresa's healing involved speaking to lawmakers, bringing awareness of human trafficking to communities, and partnering with concerned people to stop the enslavement of any human anywhere in the world.

SUMMARY

Chances of survival for victims of human trafficking are slim. Even when they escape, many are physically and psychologically damaged. Severe trauma and abuse leaves a crippling impact upon victims and requires skilled therapists. For some survivors, finding their voice and working to alleviate human trafficking can be a beneficial source of healing.

FREEDOM FIGHTERS CHALLENGE

WHAT WILL YOU DO TODAY TO HELP STOP HUMAN TRAFFICKING?

CHAPTER FIFTEEN

Q&A

AS YOU REVIEW the information from this book, here are the answers to frequently asked questions and other questions regarding human trafficking.

Q: WHAT IS THE DIFFERENCE BETWEEN A SEX SLAVE AND A VICTIM OF SEX TRAFFICKING? CAN A PERSON BE A SEX SLAVE BUT NOT BE TRAFFICKED?

A: A person can be kidnapped and held for days, months, or years and be a kidnapping victim but not a trafficking victim. A person is trafficked when there is an element of commercial sex. If an exploiter sold his sex slave to others for money, then that becomes trafficking. If a person is deceived by a job offer and instead held and sexually abused, that is trafficking. A person forced to work and not paid for it is trafficked.

Q: WERE THERESA'S TRAFFICKERS CAUGHT AND PROSECUTED?

A: No. She attempted to call the police years later but after briefly describing her story, they told her they couldn't help her. The statute of limitations was over for any hope of prosecution. In 2014, however, Michigan passed the Theresa Flores Act that permanetly removes the statute of limitations for a child victim of human trafficking, meaning that a person under the age of 18 who is trafficked can legally pursue the trafficker at any point in her life when she is ready.

Q: WHY DIDN'T THERESA'S PARENTS KNOW WHAT WAS HAPPENING TO THEIR DAUGHTER?

A: Theresa's father held a powerful position with a company that had salesmen around the world. At their annual awards ceremony, her father was honored twice with a gold ring and a trip. He traveled weekly, leaving Theresa's mom to raise the four children. Basically a single parent of the 80's, she never had to worry about financial resources, but she was lonely. Eventually Theresa's mother found interests to keep busy outside of the family, performing with the community theatre group and meeting with the Gourmet Club.

When he was home, Theresa's dad took customers to dinner, followed by drinks late into the night. Weekly, her parents dressed up and went out until the early morning hours. Theresa never doubted that her parents loved her, but they were distracted with social events, maintaining a big house in the right neighborhood, two cars, and yearly family vacations. Theresa's parents were not affectionate or emotionally attached. They were functional parents who believed in family and a strong work ethic. Children who are abused or neglected work hard to please parents. It was part of the equation that added up to a good kid from the suburbs being exploited by gang members.

The concept of human trafficking was outside the imagination of most people including Theresa's parents though they were aware that something was amiss. Most people didn't realize, and those who suspected chose not to get involved.

Q: WHAT SIGNS SHOULD HAVE ALERTED THOSE AROUND THERESA THAT SHE NEEDED HELP?

A: Teachers and trained school personnel never offered help when they observed Theresa being manipulated by an ethnic group. They saw her slammed against the locker, spit on, and harassed. Not an inner city school with metal detectors, this was a ritzy high school where most students' fathers made plenty of money. Almost daily, they watched Theresa leave with her traffickers. Unlike the kid who left early to go party after school, Theresa's eyes were dull, her head was down, and she never smiled. Flanked by two older boys, she was the picture of dread as she passed the teacher in the hall.

Q: DID THE TRAFFICKERS THREATEN THERESA OUTSIDE OF SCHOOL?

A: The traffickers frequently came into the fast food place where Theresa worked to let her know they were keeping an eye on her. Theresa was reprimanded for personal calls when they called the restaurant phone number and asked for her but when she answered, they didn't speak. They never took her from work or directly afterwards because her parents and the police could trace what time she left. They found the phone number where Theresa was babysitting and called. When they thought Theresa was being resistant, one of the men would threaten her younger brother.

Q: WHAT CAN TEENS DO TO HELP ADULTS KEEP CHILDREN SAFE?

A: Friends, family, and community members must protect children from sexual predators and molesters. Being aware and watchful is the first step.

- Ask questions, know their world, their interests.
- Know who they spend time with.
- Know where they are.
- Check to make sure they are sound asleep in their beds each night.
- Where are they going? With whom? Are they spending the night with friends and are the parents at home?
- Know the address and phone number to the place they are going. With so many teens having cell phones, parents often think they don't need another number.
- When a teen babysits, get the address and the phone number of the home where they will be.
- Take your teen to their destination.
- Pick up your teen when it is time to come home.
- Make sure your teen always carries identification.
- Be involved in school activities so you have an opportunity to view your teen in the school setting. Be aware of who interacts with your child.

- Though it may sound radical to some, occasionally visit school and sit in on class. Occasionally, drop in at their work or other activities.
- Regularly spend time one on one with your teen. Find an activity you both enjoy and listen to your teen.
- Install a security system in your home.
- Use the tracking app on your child's phone.
- Monitor your child's phone and computer history.
- Make your home the go-to place for your child and your child's friends.
- *Never* let down your guard.

Additional Resources

For additional resources go to our websites to download:

- PowerPoint slides
- Study guide and lesson plans
- Parents Guide
- Schedule Theresa Flores or PeggySue Wells to present interactive workshops at your school and community.
- Watch Theresa's documentary, "The Girl Next Door" by Andrea Picco.

ABOUT THE AUTHORS

THERESA FLORES, LSW, MS

Human trafficking survivor, best selling author, and victim's advocate, Theresa Flores is a survivor of domestic minor sex trafficking. As a 15-year-old girl in a well-to-do white suburban neighborhood, Theresa survived two years of living hell being sold to men in their 20's and 30's. She was given as a reward to men in this criminal ring when they did a good job.

An avid track runner, older sister to three younger brothers, and that all-American girl, no one, not even her parents, knew she was being trafficked.

Twenty years later, Theresa speaks out on the reality of human trafficking in the United States. She is the author of *The Sacred Bath*, *The Slave across the Street*, a *USA Today* and *Wall Street Journal* bestseller. The *Slave Across the Street* published in the UK by Random House, a top seller internationally on the UK Sunday Times list, includes a more indepth look into the escape from her traffickers and her ongoing struggle to heal.

The E-book is a #1 favorite in the categories of women's studies, child advocacy, family law, and political studies. The audio version of *The Slave Across the Street* was nominated for the 2011 Audie Award, finishing in the top five audio books for memoirs and biographies.

Theresa has been a guest on *The 700 Club*, *The Today Show*, and MSNBC's *Sex Slaves – The Teen Trade*. Founder of S.O.A.P., Theresa has also been featured on *Nightline* and *America's Most Wanted*, and *For the Record* as a sex slave survivor.

Theresa is featured by the National Underground Railroad Freedom Center Museum in a traveling exhibit entitled, *Invisible Slavery*.

As a much sought after international speaker and expert on human trafficking, Theresa was appointed to the Ohio Attorney General's Human Trafficking Commission in 2009 and testified before the Ohio House and Senate in support of Human Trafficking Legislation. Her efforts were a major part of the success of SB235 being passed into law by Ohio Governor Strickland on December 23, 2010.

Theresa has been awarded one of the top influential women in the Columbus, Ohio area. Recognized by

Ohio Governor Kasich, she received the Courage Award for her work in human trafficking.

Theresa is a licensed social worker for more than 20 years. She received her Master's in Counseling Education from the University of Dayton and a Bachelor's of Social Work from Ball State University. In October 2014, Theresa was honored to assist Michigan Governor Rick Snyder in signing the Theresa Flores Act into law that eliminates the statute of limitation for child trafficking victims.

To learn more, visit her website at:

www.traffickfree.com

PEGGYSUE WELLS

PeggySue Wells is the author of more than two dozen books, and her articles appear nationally in magazines and newspapers. An international speaker and radio co-host on award-winning WBCL, she serves as board member for RemedyLIVE, and championed Tweener Time International Teen Writing, Art, and Song Writing competition that awarded college scholarships to talented teens. She is a member of the Christian Performing Arts Fellowship, the Christian Writers Guild, Advanced Writers and Speakers Association, and Redbud Writers Guild. She writes curriculum and screenplays, conducts interactive workshops for schools, colleges, and national conferences. PeggySue ghostwrites, connects authors with publishers, writes proposals, and edits fiction and non-fiction.

PeggySue's non-fiction books include:
- *Bonding with Children Through Boundaries,* with June Hunt, Hope for the Heart, Crossway
- *Muerta de Miedo,* Unilit
- *Rediscovering Your Happily Ever After,* Kregel
- *The Slave Across the Street,* Ampelon (Audio Award finalist, #85 on *USA Today* Bestseller List, and #5 and #6 on *Wall Street Journal* Bestseller List)
- *Homecoming Kids Christmas* screenplay, Spring Hill, Gaither Productions
- *What To Do When You're Scared to Death,* Lion Hudson (international, English, Spanish, Italian)
- *What To Do When You Don't Want To Go To Church,* AMG Publishers (English, Spanish)
- *What To Do When You Don't Know What To Say To Your Own Family,* AMG (English, Spanish)
- *What To Do When You Don't Know What To Say,* Bethany House Publishers (Sold 50,000 the first year. Translated into three languages)
- *Gaither Pond Video Series Unit Studies,* Gaither Publications

- *Holding Down The Fort,* Bethany House Publishers
- *Abigail Adams: First Lady of the United States,* Purple Toad Publishers
- *Edith Wilson: First Lady of the United States,* Purple Toad Publishers
- *Soulja Boy, A Blue Banner Biography,* Mitchell Lane Publishers
- *Kanye West, A Blue Banner Biography,* Mitchell Lane Publishers
- *Fergie, A Blue Banner Biography,* Mitchell Lane Publishers

PeggySue's fiction books include:
- *Für Elise,* Elk Lake Publishers
- *The Patent,* Pegwood Publishers

PeggySue has been a columnist for the *Christian Communicator Magazine.* Her articles appear in *Focus on the Family Magazine, Clubhouse Magazine, In Touch Magazine, Significant Living, OnCourse Magazine, Church Libraries, The Advanced Christian Writer, Mature Years, Purpose Magazine, New Homeowner Magazine, New Moon Magazine, Homeschooling Today, Homecoming Magazine, ParentTalk,* and *Charisma Magazine.*

Connect with PeggySue Wells at:
www.PeggySueWells.com

RECOMMENDED RESOURCES

Films
- *Chosen*
- *Human Trafficking* with Mira Sorvino
- *In Plain Sight* staring Natalie Grant
- *Nefarious: Merchant of Souls*
- *Not My Life*
- *The Girl Next Door* by Andrea Picco
- *Trade* with Kevin Kline
- *Very Young Girls*
- *Tricked*

Books
- *The Slave Across the Street* by Theresa Flores
- *A Crime So Monstrous* by Benjamin Skinner
- *Be the Change* by Zach Hunter
- *Girls Like Us: Fighting for a world where girls are not for sale* by Rachel Lloyd
- *Half the Sky* by Nicholas Kristof
- *Not for Sale* by David Batstone

- *Renting Lacey* by Shared Hope
- *Sex Trafficking: Inside the business of modern slavery* by Siddharth Kara
- *Sold* by Patricia McCormick
- *Stolen: The true story of a sex trafficking survivor* by Katrina Rosenblatt
- *The Slave Next Door* by Kevin Bales
- *Where am I Wearing; A Global Tour to the Countries, Factories, and People that Make our Clothes* by Kelsey Timmerman
- *White Umbrella: Walking with survivors of sex trafficking* by Mary Frances Bowley and Louie Giglio

END NOTES

Chapter One

1. Meredith Dank, Bilal Kahn, P. Mitchell Downey, Cybele Kotonias, Debbie Mayer, Colleen Owens, Laura Pacifici, and Lilly Yu. "Estimating the Size and Structure of the Underground Commercial Sex Economy in Eight Major U.S. Cities," *Urban Institute*, March 12, 2014, http://www.urban.org/research/publication/estimating-size-and-structure-underground-commercial-sex-economy-eight-major-us-cities/view/full_report.

2. Ibid.

Chapter Two

1. "Human Trafficking Pie Chart," *World Resources Sim Center*, August 21, 2012, http://www.wrsc.org/attach_image/human-trafficking-pie-chart.

Chapter Three

1. Olga Khazan. "A Fascinating Map of the Worst Countries for Modern Slavery," *The Atlantic*, June 20, 2013, http://www.theatlantic.com/international/archive/2013/06/a-fascinating-map-of-the-worst-countries-for-modern-slavery/277037/.

Chapter Four

1. "Human Trafficking Pie Chart," *World Resources Sim Center*, August 21, 2012, http://www.wrsc.org/attach_image/human-trafficking-pie-chart.

ADDITIONAL RESOURCES

Heather J. Clawson, Nicole Dutch, Amy Solomon, and Lisa Gold-blatt Grace. U.S. Department of Health and Human Services. Human Trafficking into and Within United States: A Review of the Literature. August 30, 2009. http://aspe.hhs.gov/basic-report/human-trafficking-and-within-united-states-review-literature

Rosemary Regello, A Short History of Sexual Slavery, The City Edition. November 29, 2014, http://www.thecityedition.com/Pages/Archive/February/HistorySlavery.pdf.

Japan Gave G.I.'s Comfort Women, *The Australian*. November 29, 2014, http://www.theaustralian.com.au/news/world/japan-gave-gis-comfort-women/story-e6frg6so-1111113417409?nk=51df2f78e3a32a6ea942940a5cc8b1f9

Poverty and Human Trafficking, U.S. Catholic Sisters Against Human Trafficking , http://www.cscsisters.org/justice/issues/human_trafficking/Documents/USCatholicSistersModules/3_2014_ModuleonPovertyandHumanTrafficking.pdf

Kosovo, U.S. Department of State, November 29, 2014, http://www.state.gov /j/tip/rls/tiprpt/countries/2014/226755.htm Lizzie Dearden, Isis: Plea for West to help more than 1,000 kidnapped Yazidi women forced into 'sex trade', http://www.independent.co.uk/news/world/middle-east/islamic-state-plea-for -west-to-help-more-than-1000-kidnapped-yazidi-women-in-isis-sex-trade-9752220.html.

Sex Trafficking In The U.S., Polaris Project, http://www. polarisproject.org/human-trafficking/sex-trafficking-in-the-us.

Most Suspected Incidents of Human Trafficking Involved Allegations of Prostitution of an Adult or Child, Bureau of Justice Statistics, http://www.bjs.gov/ content/pub/press/cshti0810pr.cfm.

Sex Trafficking, National Human Trafficking Research Center http://www.traffickingresourcecenter.org/type-trafficking/sex-trafficking.

Elizabeth Held, Multiple forces try to break human trafficking pattern in O.C., O.C. Register, http://www.ocregister.com/articles/trafficking-525794-human-royce.html?page=1.

Susan Tiefenbrun, The Saga of Susannah A U.S. Remedy for Sex Trafficking in Women: The Victims of Trafficking and Violence Protection Act of 2000, 2002 Utah L. Rev. 116, 107 (2002).

Orange County Human Trafficking Task Force, Community Services Programs, Inc., The Salvation Army, Data collected July 2011 to Dec. 2012, Reported in the Orange County Register.

Ayla Weiss, Ten Years of Fighting Trafficking: Critiquing the Trafficking in Persons Report through the Case of South Korea,13 Asian-Pacific L. & Pol'y J. 316, 304 (2014).'

Heather J. Clawson et al, Human Trafficking Into and Within the United States: A Review of the Literature, U.S. Department of Health and Human Services (Nov. 29, 2014, 6:00 PM), http://aspe.hhs.gov/hsp/07/humantrafficking/litrev/.

Trymaine Lee, Staggering report exposes U.S. sex trafficking, MSNBC, http://www.msnbc.com/msnbc/sex-trafficking-america-0.

Trafficking of Women, Women's Stats, http://womanstats .org/newmapspage.html.

April Rieger, Missing The Mark: Why The Trafficking Victims Protection Act Fails To Protect Sex Trafficking Victims In The United States, 30 Harv. J.L. & Gender 231 (2006).

Tier Placements, U.S. Department of State, http://www. state.gov/j/tip/rls/tiprpt/2013/210548.htm

Trafficking Victims Protection Act: Minimum Standards for the Elimination of Trafficking in Persons, U.S. Department of State, http://www.state. gov/j/tip/rls/tiprpt/2011/164236.htm

Definitions and Methodology, U.S. Department of State, http://www.state.gov/j/tip/rls/tiprpt/2012/192352.htm

Pre-Court Diversion, Breaking Free, http://breakingfree. net/diversion_programs.aspx

Public Policy and Social Change, Breaking Free, http://breaking free.net/public_policy_social_change.aspx

The John School, Breaking Free, http://breakingfree.net /the_john_school.aspx

Sweden's Sexkosplagen In America, 37 Wm. Mitchell L. Rev. 1989 (2011). Sarah Orton, Sex workers in Amsterdam: Legal, but still demeaning, disturbing and degrading, The Stanford Daily, http://www.stanforddaily.com /2014/11/05/sex-workers-in-amsterdam-legal-but-still-demeaning-disturbing-and-degrading

Julie Bindel, Why even Amsterdam doesn't want legal brothels, The Spectator, http://www.spectator.co.uk/features/8835071/ flesh-for-sale/.

Hazel Thompson, Prostitution: why Swedes believe they got it right, *The Guardian*, http://www.theguardian.com/global-development/2013/dec/11/ prostitution-sweden-model-reform-men-pay-sex.

Prostitution Ban Huge Success in Sweden, Humantrafficking.org, http://www.humantrafficking.org/updates/838

Mark Kennedy, Tory government's new prostitution laws will likely target pimps, customers and sex-trade traffickers, National Post, http://news.nationalpost.com/2014/04/27/harper-governments-new-prostitution-laws-will-likely-target-pimps-customers-and-sex-trade-traffickers/#__federated

Trafficking Victims Protection Act, fighstlaverynow.org, http://fightslaverynow.org/why-fight-there-are-27-million-reasons/the-law-and-trafficking/trafficking-victims-protection-act/trafficking-victims-protection-act/.

Adelaide Mena, Pornography Seen as Root of Human Trafficking , http://www.ncregister.com/daily-news/pornography-seen-as-a-root-of-human-trafficking/.

Mary Anne Layden, Pornography and Violence: A New Look at Research, socialcostsofpornography.com, http://www.socialcostsofpornography.com /Layden_Pornography_and_Violence.pdf.